MILLER STRONG

RE-WRITE YOUR STORY.
TAKE A STAND.
TURN YOUR PAST INTO YOUR SUPERPOWER.

ERIN MILLER

Table of Contents

Forward

Sometimes it is a good thing to not know what lies ahead; to go merrily and naively through life doing all the things that good people are supposed to do, in order for everything to turn out just fine.

When Erin and I first met, we were instantly fond of each other. We worked in different areas of our small city hospital, but we seemed to be set upon a similar path, as optimistic, positive and enthusiastic women, working hard while raising our kids, participating in our community and, in general, enjoying and making the most of life.

Neither of us knew that the course of our lives was about to change drastically. Within a few short years of each other, my 24 year old daughter Amber, went missing (declared an unsolved homicide) and Erin's 21 year old son Chad, an athlete in his prime, would lose his life to a drug overdose. Neither of us were ready for this part of the journey …no parent ever is.

Countless families have suffered the devastating loss of a loved one. The grieving journey is a personal journey, and grieving timelines will vary. Families robotically navigate on autopilot, through the details and arrangements following a death, with no time to address their own grief, until the funeral is over and the company has long gone home. In Erin's case, she started the slow downward spiral into the depths of despair.

Many people are unable to find their way out. They stay stuck in this place where the grief and despair turn into anger and bitterness. Erin struggled to get herself out of this place and to get her life back and create a life that would honour her legacy. This is the story and healing journey that Erin generously shares in her book.

Like a phoenix rising from the ashes, Erin shares with you how to transform from debilitating grief and despair, to find a way to move forward with strength, determination, compassion and hope. In telling her story, Erin is determined to give hope and inspiration to you.

It has not been an easy journey. Nor will yours likely be either.

Yet, it forged Erin into who she has become today. Now, she continues to move forward on her healing journey, and shares her life wisdom to help you, dear reader, to find the path of hope toward your own healing journey.

To my dear friend Erin,

I wish health, happiness and continued healing to you and your entire family.

To those of you reading Erin's story, may you find healing, inspiration and inner peace.

Lori McFarland

Introduction

Right now, in this very moment, there are millions and millions of people going through physical, emotional, or spiritual trauma. It's highly likely that you yourself have experienced some sort of trauma, heartbreak, pain, or loss, since you purchased this book.

I believe everyone has experienced at least one moment in life where everything seemed to go against them. Life seems to be littered with these painful experiences: divorce, heartbreak, addiction, abuse, losses of loved ones, the list goes on.

And although these experiences are extremely traumatic and difficult. What I can tell you is this: hidden inside the darkest and most difficult moments of your life, there is a treasure chest with a gift locked inside. It may seem hard to believe, but once you uncover the key to your painful past, you will release a gift that becomes your superpower.

This book is about helping you find the key that unlocks the hidden gifts buried in your pain. Once you uncover these hidden gifts, you will begin the process of re-writing your own story so that it no longer enslaves you, but instead liberates you.

The hidden gifts then become the rock that you stand on. In it, your superpower will begin emerging from the traumatic moments of your life.

I know this because I have lived through sexual abuse, becoming pregnant at 15, and the devastating loss of my son to addiction. I have been slandered, maligned and falsely detained against my will. I have suffered from severe depression and PTSD. Yet, out of those horrible moments, I found my truth. I found my superpower. I became, what I call, Miller Strong.

This book is here to help you to become "Miller Strong" no matter what you have been through.

Who is this for?

You are in the right place if you have been carrying around the pain of your past for years. You are in the right place if there is something in your life that, no matter how much you try and reason through it, you just can't make sense of it. You are in the right place if you are willing to be free of heartache and finally be free.

If you have ever felt scared, alone, or isolated, this book is for you. If you suffer from depression, anxiety, or PTSD, read these pages. If someone you love died and you can't seem to forgive yourself for still being alive, then know that these pages will likely speak directly to your broken heart.

I wrote this for the seeker, the sufferer, the people who dream big, but are having a hard time believing in themselves and their own worthiness.

Who am I?

My name is Erin Miller. My entire life I have struggled to uncover who I really am. From a young age I always thought I had to prove my self-worth, because, honestly, I didn't have any. I became pregnant at 15 years old with my son Chad Miller. From that moment, my life would be different than almost every other teenager in my high school.

It motivated me to put my head down and prove, not only to myself, but others, that I would succeed. I decided I would not be left behind and I would be the best Mom I could.

Yet, my biggest trial would come when I lost my son Chad to drugs in the prime of his life. The shame, guilt, and regret haunted me for years. Eventually, I discovered how to move forward and re-write the story of our lives.

The journey has not been easy, but it is because of this that I write this book for you. Along the way I uncovered the hidden gifts locked inside of Chad's tragedy. I learned how to find my own hidden gifts. In doing so, it led me to take a stand and create the Miller Strong #17 Foundation in Chad's honor to do more good in the world and help others that struggle with addiction. In the process, I discovered my own superpower, which I will reveal to you later in the book.

Where our journey will take us

This book is part memoir and part roadmap to taking the most traumatic moments of your life and turning them into your superpower.

Through my own life story, I'll share with you the lessons, insights, and takeaways that helped me turn my life around, so you can do the same.

I believe that the most painful moments in life do not have to hold you hostage. There is a way to bypass decades of personal development and gain control over the heartache pain, abuse, addiction, loss or depression you may have experienced. This book will be your guide to get you there.

You'll learn the invaluable pathway I've discovered to take back control of your life.

Let's begin…

Chapter 1

November 19, 2014 was the day that would come to define my life.

I didn't know when I awoke on that chilly morning, that in a few hours everything about my life would be different.

I didn't know when I awoke that the events of that day would send me spiraling down a pathway of despair, heartbreak, emotional, physical, and spiritual trauma I could have never imagined.

Yet, in that darkness, my deepest life purpose would emerge.

Before I tell you what happened, you need to understand where I came from.

I am the firstborn child to my parents, George and Mona Miller. They are high school sweethearts who grew up in a tiny town in Elm Creek, Manitoba, Canada.

Like a lot of young Canadians, my Dad played hockey. He left home at a young age to play Junior A Hockey to follow his childhood dream. He moved to Portage la Prairie to play for the Portage Terriers. His team took home the Centennial Cup in 1972/73. Years later the team would be inducted into the Hockey Hall of Fame. My Mom followed him and they decided to call Portage la Prairie home.

My parents were poor when they got married. My dad didn't even have enough money to pay for his own suit at their wedding on August 10, 1974.

3 years later, on July 25, 1977, I was born in Portage la Prairie, Manitoba, a town of about 14,000 people. My brother, Curtis Miller, was born 3 years later.

We were a pretty typical Canadian family. When we were young, my mom stayed at home to raise us, while my dad worked and went to school to provide for his family. He was an entrepreneur who owned and operated an insurance company. My grandparents and extended family lived close by, so we spent lots of time with them as we were growing up. Both sets of my grandparents were always our number one fans at everything we were doing in life.

When I was younger, I was in Brownies, and I played the quintessential Canadian sport of Ringette. We were so good that our team won the Provincial Championship when I was 13. If you don't know what Ringette is, it's similar to ice hockey, but played with a straight stick and a ring instead of the normal hockey stick and puck. The rules are slightly different, but the objective is the same – score goals and win.

I was a part of the Student Council and my parents were really involved in the school activities, as well. My Dad coached my brother's hockey team, while my mom was an active volunteer for anything that needed to be done in the community or with our activities. Our family was and still is well respected and active in our community.

Growing up, I wanted to be an astronaut. Well, at least until I was in Grade 3 and a space shuttle exploded on live television, so I instantly gave up on that dream. I turned my sights on becoming a kindergarten teacher. I always thought that would be the most rewarding job in the world to introduce children to a new world and add real value to their lives.

When I was 14, I got into my fair share of trouble. My friends and I called ourselves the "North End Girls" because we lived on the north side of town. We proudly wore our tie dye shirts, trashed denim jeans, and our hair held together with a bottle of hair spray.

Like most teenagers, we tested our boundaries. We'd occasionally skip school, miss curfew, sneak out of the house, drink, smoke, and go to parties. We were just teenagers coming into our own skin and the world was ours to make what we wanted.

Or so I thought, until one day came that I'll never forget. It was in June of 1992, and my friends and I were all hanging out at our local park. There was a new boy I met at the park. We chatted for a little bit, and he asked me if I wanted to go for a walk with him to his friend's house. He seemed friendly and funny, so I said, "Sure." He was a few years older than me and seemed cool. He didn't give off any vibes to make me feel unsafe.

We walked across town, casually talking, and ended up at a two-story yellow house with a white fence. We went through the front door, and, to my surprise, nobody was there, just us. I thought his friend must have been running late or something.

It wasn't long before he started touching me and forcing himself on me. I was a 14-year-old innocent baby girl who had never had sex and had no idea of what was about to happen. He started kissing me. He tasted like old stale smoke. I tried to resist, but he kept persisting.

Before I could even get my head around what was happening, he had most of my clothes off and was on top of me, penetrating me. I was a virgin! The pain was so horrific as he kept pushing inside of me. I kept telling him to stop, that I had never had sex before, but he didn't stop. There was blood everywhere.

Finally, he said, "I can't believe you are a virgin because I was told you like to have sex, so that's why I brought you here."

I was in complete shock. Who would say that about me? Was he lying?

When he was finished, he took the bloody sheets and wrapped them up in a ball and threw them in another room. We got up, got dressed, walked back to our friends at the park as though nothing at all had happened.

As we were walking along the tracks on the way back, there was blood dripping down my legs. I could hardly walk; I was so sore. My mind was a blur. I was in excruciating pain. I felt hurt, ashamed, embarrassed, confused, and scared. I was so humiliated and wanted to know who told him that I would have sex with him.

I remember beating myself up afterwards. Asking myself, "Why did I let this happen? Maybe I am stupid to think that this wasn't where it was going? I should have known better. Why would I go with this guy that I barely knew? Why didn't I leave?

I felt that I should have stopped him, that I could have somehow done that, not understanding that I had just been a victim of sexual assault.

When we got back to the park with our friends, he acted like nothing out of the ordinary had happened.

I kept to myself at the park. I had no idea what to do. I felt dirty, disgusting, ashamed, changed, scared, alone, and so confused. One of the other boys at the gathering saw me keeping to myself and came up to me. He had brown eyes, with tan skin, and was only a few inches taller than me. I don't know what it was, but he could sense something was very off with me. It's like he knew something horrible had happened to me.

He asked, "Are you okay?"

"No, I'm not okay," I replied.

"Okay, I'm Jason," he said. "Just stay beside me. You're going to be fine."

I don't know how he knew, but it was exactly what I needed; to just be protected and feel that someone was looking out for me right then.

***

From that day on I was a different person. It's like the innocence in me just left. 25 years later, when I was doing therapy, I realized just how traumatizing that event was in my life. It affected my behavior, my self-esteem, self-worth, and self-respect. I ended up compartmentalizing this trauma my entire life. Decades later, I finally told my mom and she said she always knew something had happened to me that day. She talked to the principal that year and tried to figure out what was wrong with me. Everyone could tell I was different. My Grandfather even said to my mom that "it was like the light left her eyes that year."

It is not okay for anyone to disrespect your body – ever. If you've ever experienced rape or sexual abuse of any kind, know that you are not alone, and it is certainly not your fault. When I look back, I wish I'd had the courage to stand up for myself or to ask for help afterwards, but, like most people, I didn't know how deep the trauma was inside of me. I didn't realize how much it would shape me as a person. The shame made me pull away and ostracize myself from my family & friends and blame myself for what had happened.

If I could go back and talk to my 14-year-old self again I would say this, "Don't keep it inside. You are not alone. It's horrific, traumatizing but this happens to people all the time and it is not your fault. Get help. Speak to someone. Get the support you need. Your parents are not going to be mad or disappointed with you. They want nothing more than to protect you. Forgive yourself and you need to heal because I absolutely did not deserve this abuse."

It takes courage to talk about topics like this, but when you do, you are taking a stand for yourself and what you know is right in the world. It creates change bigger than you can imagine when you shine light on these tragedies, so that this doesn't happen to more people.

Chapter 2

After Jason gave me the safety and protection I needed on that horrible day, I was drawn to him. He made me feel safe. We started hanging out a lot and I liked being around him. He was always making people laugh - including me. He was incredibly talented at music. He played the guitar and had a powerful singing voice. He eventually became my boyfriend.

So, there I was, a 15-year-old girl, in grade 10, dating an older boy who didn't go to school or work. He lived at home with his Mom. I went from being a regular teenager who was on sports teams and school council, to a whole other world and focus with Jason.

But that wasn't the only thing that changed for me. In December of 1992, I noticed I was getting violently ill and vomiting every day. I felt exhausted all the time. And then I missed my period. Oh God, really?

Yes.

I was pregnant.

I tried to hide the morning sickness as much as I could, but my mom started questioning me a lot.

"Are you okay, Erin?" she would ask. "Have you been sexually active?"

"No, mom! I'm fine!" I acted like it was no big deal. What teenager wants to tell their parents that they're pregnant or sexually active?

At that point, I'd missed a few periods and I knew I was definitely pregnant, even if I didn't want to admit it to myself. Although I hadn't confessed anything to her, my mom made an appointment for me to go see our family doctor, Dr. Antonissen.

I went to the appointment alone. I remember peeing in the cup and handing it to the nurse. After a short wait, the doctor came back in the patient room and said to me, "Erin, you're pregnant. You're 15 years old, I will need to contact your Mom and we will all get together again next week and talk about this together."

I left the clinic unsurprised; in some ways relived that he was going to tell my Mom. I felt scared but I also felt blessed. I was going to be a Mom, and I knew I was going to be an awesome one at that. I knew it wasn't going to be easy, but I had that excitement and absolute fear mixture that I think most women have when they unexpectedly find out they're pregnant.

The hardest part was facing all of my friends and family to let them know. As I gradually told the people in my life, I could see the disappointment, the shame, the judgment and the fear everyone had for me. I was going to have a baby and there was no happiness nor congratulations. I felt little love or support from my family and most of my friends.

When I told Jason, he didn't know what to do. He started talking frantically. "How could this be happening? We were not very careful. I knew this was going to happen! Maybe it's a mistake? I'm going to be a Dad! What are we going to do?"

Our entire lives had changed and we both knew it.

"Is this possible? I mean, this is crazy. Is this really happening?" he stammered.

"Uh, yeah, of course it's really happening." I didn't know what to say. "I have to start making plans to be a Mom!"

The look on his face was pure fear. We both knew my parents would be disappointed.

Telling my parents I was pregnant at 15 was one of the most difficult conversations of my life. To top it off, they were not fans of Jason. He was a few years older than me and a high school dropout. My Mom was worried, naturally, that things weren't going to be okay. She was afraid that I would be left behind, unable to finish high school.

I was scared and too proud to ask my parents for their help during the pregnancy. I felt I could do this on my own and I wasn't sure they were going to support me, so I decided to move out of the house. I remember telling them, "I don't really need your help. I'll be fine." I was trying to convince myself as much as I was trying to convince them. The truth was I was scared to death.

I packed a bag and went to Jason's mom's house where he lived in a basement bedroom. His mom certainly was not welcoming to me. His family was very poor. They had no food.

Jason's life was very different from mine. In his family, there was lying, cheating, fighting, drinking, drugs, physical, emotional and sexual abuse. And serious control issues that I hadn't noticed before.

Before long, Jason started controlling who I could spend my time with. I started to believe he was the only person I could trust. He quickly put a wedge between my old life and the life we were living together. I would visit my parents, but they had no idea how bad things were. They had no clue that I didn't even have food and that my life was regularly in jeopardy. Jason's brother stole from me and he even threw me in front of a car once. It was a nightmare.

The longer I stayed, the lower my self-esteem went. I had no guidance and I accepted that this was what my life was going to be like. By this point Jason was manipulating me and getting very jealous of every relationship I had with anybody. He told me what I could and couldn't do. He had no job, no money, we barely ate, it was horrible. I didn't want to be a single Mom. I wanted us to be a family and, in my innocence, I trusted that things would get better.

***

I got a babysitting job and I worked as much as I could to stash every penny. On my lunch breaks I would go to parenting classes a few times a week. So between trying to go to school, babysitting to save money and taking my prenatal classes, things were really busy.

Everyone at school started to look at me differently, especially once I began to show. I could feel the other students and teachers judging me. Certain teachers seemed to put less effort into me. It was like they thought my future wasn't as bright as the other kids, so I wasn't worth investing the same amount of time and energy into. Thank goodness for the few who could see that I needed some extra help.

The conversation of adoption came up a few times. I remember my Mom took me to Winnipeg to meet with an Adoption Agency. I didn't want to go, but I was 15 and I had to get all the options, so I went anyway. When I got there the lady from the organization started asking me questions about Jason.

"So, how aboriginal is he? How aboriginal do you think your child is going to be?" she asked. There was a not-so-well-hidden hint of disdain in her voice.

I was shocked. Could someone really be that racist?

I literally threw my glass of water across the table at the woman and stormed out of the room.

"How dare you take me to a place like this!" I screamed at my mom.

She didn't know the lady would ask that, but I was just so furious. It was the first time I learned about prejudice and how my child's life was valued differently because he was going to be aboriginal.

From then on, any ideas of giving up my child for adoption went out the window.

***

Fortunately, by the time I was almost ready to deliver in August of 1993, I had been able to reconnect and develop a better relationship with my parents. They were very worried about me.

And they had every right to be. I was 15 years old, alone, pregnant, living under a roof with an abusive boyfriend who didn't contribute. Even though I felt unworthy, and that I had disappointed everyone, including myself, I still always felt blessed to be giving birth to my boy.

I remember feeling like I was going into pre-labor. I was with Jason at the time. He called my mom to come pick me up. She took me back to her house as the labor was starting. It was too early to go to the hospital, but I remember lying in bed agonizing as the pain increased. I thought I was going to die it was so intense. Nobody can prepare you for this feeling. Around 1 in the morning, I said to my mom, "I think we need to go to the hospital."

I wasn't ready to give birth. I didn't really want to in that moment. I was scared. But when the delivery ball gets rolling there's not much use trying to stop it.

We got in the car and picked up Jason on the way to the hospital.

The actual labor seemed to take an exceptionally long time. The pain management was horrible. I could feel almost everything. I was screaming and crying, the pain was so intense. Jason was losing it seeing me go through this pain. He couldn't stay in the room. My mom had to step in and be there for me, coaching me through the contractions alongside the nurses.

Despite the pain, my beautiful boy, Chad Miller, was born into this world, weighing 7 pounds 11 ounces. He was healthy and strong. I was instantly in love. I'd never seen anything more perfect in my entire life. I instantly fell in love.

Chapter 3

I spent a few days in the hospital recovering with him, and then it was time to take my baby boy home to Jason's sister's house, Michelle. She was more than happy to take us all into her home!

When we were getting ready to go, one of the nurses asked me, "Can I look at your car seat? We'll need to check it out before you are released."

"Uh, I don't have a car seat," I responded. "I've got a stroller though. I don't have a car or my driver's license yet."

They didn't like that, but I ended up convincing them to let me take him home in a stroller.

That first night at home I hardly slept. I was worried all night long that something was going to happen to him. Every little noise he made woke me up for the few moments that I fell asleep. But despite my exhaustion, I had never been more in love with anything in my entire life. And that would never ever change.

***

It was four weeks before I went back to school. Being back in school so soon, having to support myself and work, and putting Chad in daycare was brutal.

In fact, it was almost unheard of for someone my age with a newborn child to even consider putting their child in daycare, so I had to get a special government exemption to be able to get permission for him to attend daycare that young. I also applied for subsidized daycare, because I simply couldn't afford regular daycare. Even with the subsidy, I could barely cover the $2.40 per day it cost for Chad to be there, but I knew I needed to make it work because I had to get back to finishing high school on time.

Because I was heading back to school, I also could not breastfeed him, plus I didn't feel comfortable with idea anyway. So, I had to pay for formula on top of all of the other things while trying to sandwich time for school, my job, and being a brand-new mom. In the beginning Jason tried but he never contributed a dollar, so I couldn't count on him.

I tried my best to do what I could to get by. Someone told me I should go apply for welfare. I remember thinking, "What's welfare?"

I went down to the government building and chatted with a lady behind a big glass screen.

"I'm here to talk to you about welfare," I said.

She looked at me confused. "How old are you?"

"I'm 16," I said.

"I'm sorry, honey, you have to be 18 to be on welfare," she said.

I tried to convince her to give me some sort of exemption, but she said it was out of her hands. I had to figure out something fast, so I could provide for Chad. A friend told me about the Salvation Army, so I went there and one of the workers gave me food stamps.

After I got the food stamps, I remember going to Safeway with Chad and Jason, so I could get the formula, diapers, and a little bit of food for myself. I was trying to figure out how much food stamps were worth, so I could pay for everything.

We were standing in the checkout line, and I was feeling completely overwhelmed with trying to figure all of this out. I was losing hope, feeling that I might be in over my head. I knew that Jason wasn't going to pay for a thing and that I'd been doing this parenting thing basically on my own. I was so frustrated standing in that line, knowing my life had gone a direction I didn't plan on, when all of the sudden a woman standing behind me changed my life forever.

I was about to hand over my food stamps to pay for everything once the cashier rang it up – I honestly hoped that I had enough – when the lady behind me stopped me.

"You hang on to those, Dear " she said. "I'm paying for all of this. You go back and get the exact same thing, so you can have extra and you will never be working from behind. You will always be ahead."

I broke into tears and I hugged her I said, "Thank you! You have no idea how much I need this!"

Looking back I'm sure she could see how much I needed it. To this day I am forever grateful, and I don't even know her name. I didn't know what to say or do. In that moment, when I felt that absolutely every system, every relationship, my parents, Jason, my school, everything was failing me as I tried to keep my head afloat, to provide for myself and my son trying to go to school to better provide for us this woman stepped in and gave me a chance and I didn't even know her.

From then on, I knew I could do absolutely anything. A complete stranger made me realize that it was okay to start asking for help, so I started. I began asking people for help, because, honestly, I needed it.

Sometimes our pride gets in the way. Sometimes we think we can handle all of it ourselves. Sometimes we give ourselves brownie points for facing the obstacles alone. But we all need help sometimes. You'll never get it if you don't raise your hand and ask. So put your pride aside and allow yourself to be helped. It feels good to help another human in need. Don't deprive someone else of giving you that opportunity. From that moment, I've always gone out of my way to give someone else a chance or opportunity , especially when they don't seem like they deserve it…because that's probably when they need it the most.

Chapter 4

In October, Jason, Chad and I temporarily moved into my parents' house. My Mom and I made a bed for Chad out of a suitcase. Everyone had finally accepted the reality and was working together for the best. They helped us get on our feet.

In January, we moved into a one-bedroom apartment. Jason eventually got a job at a local farm. I was in grade 11 and my parents were providing a lot of emotional support. I got my driver's license and my first car – a bright orange Mercury Topaz that we named "The Bomb."

Shortly after that, life dropped a huge "bomb" on me. I couldn't believe it, but I was pregnant AGAIN. I was devastated and in complete shock. This time there was no way I could have this child. I was already barely keeping my head above the water financially. Even though Jason had a job, he wasn't contributing. The idea of having a second child at this time was completely overwhelming. I made the difficult decision to have an abortion.

This was by far the hardest decision of my life. I simply felt I didn't have a choice. I went to the doctor and when I was almost 3 months pregnant, I had an abortion. I certainly couldn't tell anyone. Jason knew and that was it.

As I walked into the Hospital to have the abortion, a lady came running up to me and asked me if I knew by going in there that I was killing my child. I remember replying that, "I simply do not have a choice." She said, "You always have a choice." I told her this was the hardest decision I will ever have to make in my life.

I remember thinking, "Erin you can never regret this because today this is the best you can do for yourself and when this is done you need to forget about it."

It was one of the worst days of my life.

As you can imagine, that year my relationship with Jason deteriorated quickly. To top it off, he had an addiction problem and became increasingly more violent.

I remember coming home one evening after dropping my Mom and her friend off at the train station. He was drinking, and he got really loud and aggressive when I told him I was with my Mom. He didn't believe me. He was a jealous mess. I tried to pick up the phone and call for help, but he ripped the phone out of the wall as he screamed at me, threatening to choke me with the phone cord. He spit in my face and told me he was going to throw me down the stairs. I've never felt so scared in my life.

I knew I had to get Chad and myself out of that apartment. I called my Dad the next day and asked if I could move home. He said, "Of course." I asked my good friend Rodney Slater to come pick me and Chad up that evening. While Jason was out, I packed up everything we needed. Rodney came and got us and took us to my parent's house. I was so relieved because now I knew I was going to be okay and the abusive nightmare was over.

Or so I thought. After Jason realized I'd left, he started terrorizing me, threatening to kill me. He told me his detailed plan on how he was going to kidnap Chad. I wanted to move out of town, but I didn't have the money to do so. I just needed to protect Chad.

It got so bad that I had to get restraining orders against Jason. Everyone was on high alert - especially the daycare. They were worried that Jason would storm in and take Chad. So, I had to do what was best for my son and start my new life without Jason. I got full custody and focused on raising the best son I could.

***

With my family reunited, we moved to a bigger house that had 2 bedrooms in the basement, so Chad and I would have our own space. Things started to become more stable. Chad became a big part of my family's life with us living under one roof.

My brother and his friends would hang out with Chad and looked at him as a little brother. My Mom helped me be a parent. We all started working together to make the best life possible. Bit by bit, it started to feel like I was finally winning.

My time at school was the only real time I felt like I was still a teenager. It was a brief relief from the constant pressure of being a teenage mom. In June of 1995, I graduated high school. This was a huge accomplishment for me to graduate on time and I was so proud of myself.

After that, I was ready to enter the work force full time. Delnora Rice hired me to work as a Dietary Aide at the Portage District General Hospital. I always felt like she gave me a chance. I had no qualifications and a two-year-old son. Yet, she still hired me! I was excited that I would actually have my own money for the first time in my life!

I'll never forget my first day on the job. I walked in scared wearing a golden dress with pantyhose, my hair in a hair net and runners on my feet. The place was chaotic. Everyone was running around like crazy people. It was the Foundation Friday BBQ (ironically, years later I was in charge of that same BBQ serving 1000 people). The cook was having loads of food for the event. There was so much going on that no one had time to train me.

I remember one of the cook's coming up and saying, "I need you to make a bunch of egg salad sandwiches."

I didn't even know what an egg salad sandwich was. I definitely didn't know how to make it. I scrambled around trying to get advice from my co-workers on how to do it as they rushed around trying to get food made. I'm sure they were wondering why they would hire someone that doesn't even know what an egg salad sandwich is. It was Darlene Tessier that could see me struggling. She came to me and assured me things would get better and she would show me the way!

My first few weeks on the job were pretty comical. I learned how to use a dishwasher, which I'd never used before. My mom always did that.

Despite the steep learning curve, the people that I worked with were incredible. They were kind hearted, open, and generous. They took me in and welcomed me into their community when so few other people in my life were doing that. To this day I'm still friends with most of the women that I worked with.

Everyone cared about each other. Work was legitimately fun. We'd laugh a lot and joke around with each other. It was a very stabilizing time in my life after my difficult high school years.

Chapter 5

In 1996, a year or so after I started working in the kitchen, change came knocking once again.

One night, I went out with some friends to a local bar called Club West. We were having drinks. The DJ was spinning music and we were all having a great time. They were running a contest that evening for some grand prize and the DJ called out, "And the winner is Erin Miller!"

Oh my God! I was so excited! Everyone was cheering as I ran up on stage. Once I got up there the DJ looked at me with a bit of confusion. He said, "You're Darren Miller?"

"Oh! I thought you called Erin Miller? I'm Erin!" I replied.

We had a good laugh about it. While I didn't win the grand prize, I did catch the attention of the DJ. His name was Ryan. He was tall with soft brown eyes and brown hair. He was handsome. He chatted with me later that evening. There was definitely a spark between us, so we started hanging out a little bit. Then we started hanging out a lot. Then it turned into something serious.

Eventually, we ended up moving in together. It made sense for us. We both had a child from another relationship, so we made our own mixed family together. His son Tyler would come and stay with us for a month at a time and then go back to live with his mom that lived out of Province.

Ryan was kind and made me feel safe. He loved to travel, and he opened my eyes to adventure and going to new places. Eventually, we decided to have a child of our own. Chad was around 4 years old at the time when I got pregnant and I wanted him to have a sibling.

Our sweet baby girl Kaeley was born on April 24, 1998. It was nice to be ready for the birth experience this time. I felt excited, supported and prepared. We had everything ready for her to arrive. She had her own room set up with a crib ready to go. It was wonderful to go through the pregnancy having Ryan's support all along the way. Chad fell in love with his little sister immediately. He protected her and looked out for her.

While our family continued to grow, I noticed that Chad's passions started to develop as he got older. He loved hockey and wanted to play it any chance he could get. Fortunately, Ryan's brother played in the NHL. His name is Reid Simpson, a famous hockey player at the time, and as soon as Chad was old enough to know about hockey he looked up to Reid. Anytime Ryan got to go see his brother play hockey he'd take Chad along with him. It was a dream come true for a Canadian boy being able to hang out with living NHL stars.

As the kids got older the demands on my time got bigger and bigger. I had to change jobs so Ryan and I could fit the kids into our schedules. I ended up taking a housekeeping position at the hospital. It was brutal, exhausting, physical work. The winters in Manitoba are terrible and all the sidewalks are constantly covered in sand. People track it in and out of the hospital all day long, so I was constantly cleaning the floors just to keep things under control.

After about 3 years of doing that job, I'd had enough. I remember one Christmas I had to get the kids up and do Christmas with them before I had to be at work at 8am on Christmas Day. That was it. I said to myself, "I'm not doing this anymore. I'm going to find a different job."

Literally, a few days later I saw a job posted in the hospital for an Operating Slating Clerk position. It was Monday to Friday from 10am-2pm. "Oh my God," I thought. "This is perfect, I will never have to miss any of the my kids activities ever again!" However, everyone I told I was interested in the job thought I was crazy to apply because it was a brand new position with a lot of unknowns.

So, I went and found out more about what this new position was going to be about. I quickly learned it was going to evolve as time went on. That was perfect for me as I am a dreamer and not scared to work. I was up for the challenge and knew I needed to be doing something else. So I took the chance and jumped in.

To this day, I see people holding themselves back from incredible opportunities, adventures, and experiences. All because someone told them (or they told themselves) that they were not qualified to do that or they didn't have enough information. Passion, persistence, hard work and confidence are some of the most valuable qualities you can possess. With them, you'll figure out how to become "qualified" for the position, or how to get yourself ready for the experience. I'm glad I did. It shaped the rest of my life.

It ended up being one of the best experiences of my career. I shaped that place and spent over 10 years working there. These incredible driven women took me under their wings and taught me a lot. The team taught me about work ethic, contribution to community, compassion and how to stick up for yourself. They built up my confidence and made me feel like a big part of the team!

Chapter 6

Chad has always been an amazing kid. As he moved into his teenage years I could really see who he was becoming as a young man. Those qualities really began to shine. He was funny, quick witted, and charismatic – a real charmer. People everywhere just loved him and he would rally people together and get them all having a great time. He was everyone's best friend and had a million-dollar smile.

Of course, he wasn't without his share of mistakes. After all, he was still a teenager.

I remember one time when he was 15, Chad and his whole hockey team decided to egg another kid's house. If you don't know what that is, it's when a bunch of people grab uncooked eggs and throw them at someone's house. Yup, the entire house covered in egg yolks and the lawn covered in egg shells - definitely not a fun thing to clean up.

After it happened, the parents knew that the hockey team had done it. Yet, they blamed Chad Miller entirely for being the one who instigated it and did the deed. Chad took responsibility for it and owned it. He didn't rat out any of the other hockey players, even though he could have.

Sure, he makes mistakes and does stupid things like we all do, but he owned them. That's one of my favorite qualities about him.

Another time, his class was on a trip for the volleyball team. He snuck beer on to the bus. Obviously, I wasn't happy that he did it, but, Chad and his buddy Jamie Kirkland took responsibility and had to make a video about drinking on a school bus as a consequence.

Even though Chad had a great relationship with his step-father Ryan, he could never fully take over the role of father for him. Chad struggled deeply with how bad of a Dad his real father Jason was. Jason was basically non-existent and that hurt Chad badly. Chad would pour in to the pages of his journal his frustrations and anger with his real father. He felt betrayed. He couldn't understand how someone could just leave their kid and not even attempt to contact them for years.

He would compare his life to his friends. He was jealous of his friends that had their biological father's in their lives, that would come to their hockey games, and seemed to care about what they were doing. This underlying pain drove Chad on the hockey rink and, honestly, is probably one of the reasons he was so good and loved to be the life of the party for everyone else. Deep down, I'm sure he was seeking his own sense of love, because he just couldn't understand how a father would not care about his own son.

There are millions of people struggling with this same issue today. Single mothers raising boys the best that they can, but many of these boys are angry and frustrated, hurt, abandoned and feeling alone. They can't understand how the one man who was supposed to be there for them and be their example of what it means to be a man, has betrayed them.

I honor the step-fathers like Ryan who boldly step into a disjointed family like that and do their very best to be a male role model for their stepsons – even when those stepsons don't want anything to do with them. It's difficult ground to tread on for everyone, but one whose story has to be told, then re-written, and healed.

***

As Chad and Kaeley grew older, their relationship only grew sweeter. Chad always included her in whatever he was doing. He was really proud of her and she was proud of him. She'd follow him all over the province to watch him play hockey, baseball, football, and golf. She became Chad's number one fan.

Kaeley was a real trooper because she'd get car sick very easily. I felt terrible for her and I committed to figuring out how to fix it. I don't remember how I came up with it, but I figured out that if she sat on a paper bag in the car, she wouldn't get sick. It sounds strange, but it worked – and that's all I cared about!

Unfortunately, as the kids got older, Ryan and I grew more and more distant. As a radio DJ during the day and a DJ in the evenings and weekends at various bars and clubs, he was gone a lot. We tried to make it work, but eventually it just made sense for us to go our separate ways. In 2011, we decided to get a divorce.

That was really difficult. Especially living in a small town where everyone knows your business. They all want to talk and know what's going on. Everyone has an opinion about your life. The people that were close to us were not surprised because they knew things had not been fine for years. We had friends that picked sides, but there were no sides to pick. This was a mutual agreement that should have been made many years before. We were not in love with each other. We just went on living but not loving each other.

This is where I see a lot of marriages fail. They get comfortable. They get complacent. They drift away from each other. They stop growing. And if you're not growing, you are dying. Passion fades away. Growth stops. The focus goes from one another to children, life, and career. You stop appreciating each other and one day you wake up and realize that your are roommates. All humans want LOVE, respect, care and compassion. We want to have someone that is in total love with you and everything about you. And we want to feel the same for someone else.

There are two pieces of advice I always taught Chad and Kaeley.

First: Treat people the way you want to be treated.

Second: What you want in a relationship is that you both think you are the luckiest one. If you both think you're the luckier one, it means its golden and it will work.

When Ryan and I split, Chad was already out of the house at college in North Dakota. Kaeley was 13 at the time. Since we owned a home together, Ryan decided to move out, so it wouldn't be as much of a drastic change for her.

Chad never said a lot about it, but I know it was painful for him when we split. It hit Kaeley particularly hard. She was very traumatized by the whole experience. Living in a town of 14,000 people, everyone knows your business. Her classmates were not shy about gossiping about it. It wasn't as common as it is today for parents in our town to get a divorce. She had a hard time with it.

I remember having multiple conversations about it with her, trying to help her understand. I told her, "This has nothing to do with you. This is just between your father and me." But it's hard for a kid to understand. Their once stable world is all of the sudden completely different.

On top of that, our household income was cut in half since we were now separate and paying for our own things. It was difficult to be a single parent again with all the responsibilities on my shoulders.

For anyone who is going through something like this, whether as a parent or a child you know this. There are always things in life that are out of your control. You can't always do something to reverse the events that have happened. Their behavior doesn't reflect on you. But what it does do is allow you to take control of what you can control.

You can control the story you tell about the experience. You can control what you choose to believe. You can control how you decide to live. You can control your decision to still keep a relationship with your parents or your children, instead of shutting down.

And parents, please remember that your kids are battling with their own struggle when you split. They need you more than ever during this time. I see so many kids being emotionally left behind as parents split up and they find their own lives. The children seem to be somewhat left behind. They don't know where they belong, so it is our job as parents to ensure they have the support they need.

I believe that, in general, people are trying to do the best with what they have been given.

So ask yourself…

"Are you doing the best you can with what you've been given?"

If the answer is no, then learn from it and begin to change. Maybe you've been dealt a really terrible hand at life. Maybe your Mom or Dad doesn't live with you anymore, but are you going to choose to do the best you can with what is? Figure out what else you can do to make it better, because you can't change the situation that someone else gives you.

If the answer is yes, then do your best to accept it and move forward. That's all you can do. Treat people the way you want to be treated going forward. Always do that. Stand up for someone else if you feel you weren't stood up for. If you see someone going through a divorce or a family breaking apart, have empathy. We all go through horrible things. Are you going to choose to pile more crap on the situation or are you going to choose to be a force for good?

I've found one of the best ways to do this is to look at that person and try my best to put myself in their shoes.

I ask myself, "If I were in their exact situation could I see myself acting similarly?"

Or, if I'm having a hard time seeing from their perspective, I'll ask myself, "What would it have taken for me to get into a space where I think or act similar to them?"

We all have the capacity to behave a certain way if enough things go the right or wrong way. The problem happens when we think we're immune to what happens to other people. We lose our humanity in the process.

Chapter 7

As much as I would've loved for Chad to roll through his final year in high school without issue, that was not to be the case.

I'll never forget. In grade 12, he called me one evening and said, "Mom, you'll never guess what just happened to me. I just saw a text that coach sent to the other players. I got kicked off the hockey team!" He was the Captain of the team and they'd just finished playing in the all-star-game. It was devastating to him.

Chad and his coach had had a few disagreements before. There was a perfect clash of personalities that had been building up for months only to have the straw that broke the camel's back be something trivial.

Chad got kicked off of the team, apparently, for shooting pucks at the net after the whistle blew. The whole thing a mess of personalities and politics. Needless-to-say, Chad was happy to be going off to school and to get out of the small-town drama.

He went off to school in Bottineau North Dakota to study and play hockey and baseball at Dakota College. I remember dropping him off. No matter what anyone tells you beforehand, it's a painful and sad thing for a mother to be taking her baby off to school.

The first semester at college went well for Chad. It was a very liberating experience for him to be away from Manitoba. He seemed like he was finding himself and getting away from the judgement and politics that he'd felt back home. Like most college kids, it was his first time being on his own. He loved travelling around the States playing hockey.

Unfortunately, it didn't last long. The rules for playing sports at the junior level in North Dakota changed during that first year, and they weren't allowed to take on as many international players.

Ryan's brother, Reid Simpson, had just purchased the Illiana Blackbirds Junior hockey team and invited Chad out to their camp and try outs in Indiana. He made the cut. It was exciting and proud times for our whole family.

It was amazing to watch. In a way, it felt like his dreams were coming true. Chad was always an amazing hockey player. Everyone said he had amazing hands. Growing up in Canada, it's almost every boys dream to go to the NHL and having the opportunity to move up through the junior league , it looked like everything was on the right track.

Two of his other friends from back home in Portage la Prairie, Josh Pashe and Damon Reeves, also got invited to play on the team in Indiana, so the three friends went off to play together.

Chad moved in with what's called a "billet family." Basically, they're families who open up their homes for junior hockey players during the season. They provide housing and support the young men that have left their hometowns to play high level hockey.

The Nisevich were the name of the family. Karen and Nick were the parents, with their two kids Jenna and Alex. And now with Chad in the home, it was a full house of 5.

I'll be honest, it was hard for me to be away from Chad and I struggled with my identity back in Portage. I mean, I'd always been "Chad Miller's Mom" up until he left for the States. I was excited when I got the chance to go watch him play in Indiana and meet his billet family .

I immediately fell in love with the Nisevich's family. They were a lot like me and Ryan before things deteriorated. Their house was full of love, laughs, shenanigans, and just being silly. Karen and I had an instant connection. It was like we were soul-sisters or something.

Chad rolled his eyes and smiled when he saw how Karen and I connected. He wasn't even homesick because she was basically like me.

Chad had always been an incredible leader on and off the ice, and this was no different. People came to cheer the team on and they'd have all these signs with Chad Miller's name on it. It made me so proud to hear them cheer him on as he stacked up goals on the scoreboard. You couldn't miss him on the ice. And when he was off the ice, everyone knew it too.

Walking around Indiana, I'd run into people and they'd say, "Oh, hey, I was at your son's hockey game tonight. Amazing!"

Everything was going incredibly well for Chad. He was playing well. He was getting the attention he wanted and making his mark in the hockey league. He finished his first year winning the runner up MVP of the year for the league and he made the All-Star Team as a rookie. He was quickly making connections in the industry. He called me and told me one day his jersey would be going up in the rafters – his dreams were coming true. He even was hanging out with stars like Kid Rock, Chris Chelios & Eddy Vetter. The future looked very bright for him and I couldn't have been prouder.

Chapter 8

Since we lived in Manitoba, I couldn't make all of his games in person, so I watched most of them online where they were streamed. My mom and I were watching one of the last games of the season online and doing things around the house. The internet connection that day wasn't great. It was cutting in and out. The stream reconnected and I remember thinking, "Where's Chad?" He hadn't been on the ice for a little while.

Well, Ryan had gone down to watch Chad play in person. Ryan was so proud of him and loved to go to his games even though we weren't together any more.

The phone rang.

"Hello?"

"Hey." It was Ryan. "I've got bad news. Chad separated his shoulder. He'll be fine, but they had the paramedics and the doctor come set it back in place. He'll be okay, they say."

"I want to talk to him," I said. I was worried.

"Chad, are you okay?" I asked.

"I'm fine, mom. It's no big deal."

I didn't believe him, but what could I say. He'd always been the type to power through injuries.

When he was in grade four his appendix burst and they had to rush him into the operating room for an emergency surgery. He almost died. He took the whole thing like a champion. The nurses said, "He's a really strong kid, because most people don't survive what he just went through."

He'd made it through that, so I figured a dislocated shoulder wouldn't keep him down for too long.

The hockey season was wrapping up, and I called Karen, Chad's billet mother in Indiana. Something seemed off with Chad the last few times I'd talked to him since the injury. He was supposed to be making plans to come back to Manitoba for the summer, but he was being really flaky about the whole thing. I needed to know if Karen could tell me anything.

"Erin," she said. "This is a bad situation. Chad was given Vicodin."

"What's that?" I asked. I honestly didn't know.

"It's a medication they gave him for the pain, but it's very addictive." Karen was an emergency nurse. She explained to me how it had become an addiction epidemic in the US.

This was in 2013, and I had no idea that the US was in the middle of an opioid crisis. It hadn't come to our small town in Manitoba, yet. I started researching Vicodin and reading everything I could find about it. What I discovered was terrifying. I read account after account of people getting seriously addicted to the pain medications.

I knew he could not be taking them. Chad has always had the type of personality that was "all in." That quality made him a great athlete, but I knew it would be a bad thing for him with the medication. I read horrible stories about the side effects of it and how it affected people's health, relationships and financial situations. He had battled addiction with drugs and alcohol while he was in high school. I knew this was a bad thing.

I couldn't figure out why in the world someone would give this highly addictive medication to a 20-year-old boy. From everything I read, Vicodin was for severe pain. I didn't think that's what he was experiencing. To top it off, it contains opioids. Even though it's legal, I had a bad feeling about it.

Chad came home for the summer. We agreed that he couldn't be on the medication, because for whatever reason, his body kept wanting more and more of it. He spent the summer hanging with his old friends and recovering. He seemed like he was getting better and stronger, so eventually it was time to go back to Indiana.

The second year back, he moved in with a different billet family. This time it was Chad and another player from Russia that lived together.

Everything seemed to be going fine. Chad was playing hockey and doing well – not as well as the year before - but he seemed to be doing good. I noticed he seemed a bit less engaged when I talked to him, but I didn't think it was anything to be overly concerned about.

In January, I got a phone call from Ryan.

"Chad's gotten himself into trouble. He's gotten mixed up with drugs."

"What do you mean?" I said.

"He got arrested, along with his roommate. They were trying to buy heroin and got busted."

I didn't know what to say. I was in complete shock. I was mad at him, concerned for him, and mad at myself, all at the same time. How did I get so out of the loop? I realized I had no idea what was going on with him.

Apparently, someone had set them up and they'd gotten busted. Chicago was cracking down hard on heroin because it was becoming such a problem. Since Chad and his roommate tried to buy the drugs, but didn't actually take possession of them, they spent a night in jail and were released the next day.

When I got the chance to talk to Chad on the phone the entire conversation was strange. He was evasive. He gave me a story about how he got set up, but he didn't say much. He promised me he wasn't doing heroin and wasn't going to. I believed him because I wanted to believe that he'd never do that, that he was smarter than that. I wanted to put all of this behind us.

The coaches assured me that they'd keep an eye on him. Chad went back to playing hockey for the next couple of months and finished up the season strong, breaking all sorts of records that year. I was optimistic that things would be alright.

He came home in March and got a job for a little bit. I noticed he was different. Just the way he looked was different. He looked like he'd lost a lot of weight. I asked him about it and he said, "I'm just getting in better shape."

While Chad lived in Indiana, he'd met a girl that he'd become really serious with. Her name was Jamie. We'd met her a few times and the whole family loved her. That summer she came up to Canada to visit Chad for a few weeks. Jamie was the love of his life. The two of them were smitten with each other. It warmed my heart to see the two of them together.

After the summer, Chad decided that he wanted to go to Chicago, even though his time in the junior hockey league had come to an end. He'd spent the last few years building a community of friends there, and the thought of not being with Jamie was terrible to him. He couldn't relate to the people back in Portage anymore.

But when he told me this, I got worried. I didn't believe that he was going to be okay in Chicago. I had that gut feeling mother's get when they know something is not good for their children.

In fact, I had a conversation with Chad and my Mom and I said to him, "If you go to Chicago you will be coming home in a body bag. I cannot support or help you."

This was tough love because I knew how badly he wanted to go and I knew how close he was to making it prior to separating his shoulder. But I had to convey to him the severity of the situation.

It didn't help that earlier in the year when I'd gone down to watch Chad play in the playoffs that I had a conversation with his teammate's father. He was a lawyer that helped Chad when he got arrested.

I'll never forget. We stood on the sidelines watching the players skate up and down the ice, when he asked me, "Erin, can I give you some advice?"

"Of course," I replied.

"Now that Chad has done heroin – I hate to say this – but you can never fully trust him again...ever. He tried it. And it doesn't matter if he tried it one time or a hundred times...you can't trust him." He turned his head and looked at Chad skating by on the rink. He looked back at me and said, "This stuff takes over people's lives."

I didn't want to believe him when he told me that, but in my gut, I knew there was truth to it. When I got back to Manitoba, I spent days researching heroin, how it affects the body, and how addicting it is.

Everything I read was horrible. I was so worried for him. But what happened next, I could never have prepared for.

Chapter 9

In the fall of 2014, Chad was enrolled in Robert Morris University where he would play hockey for the Eagles in Chicago. I pleaded with him not to leave, but he wouldn't listen. I didn't want him back in that environment. I couldn't protect him from that far away. But, honestly, what could I do? He was a 21-year-old man at that time. As much as I hated it, he legally didn't have to listen to me.

This was tough love from me because I knew how bad he wanted to succeed with hockey, and I wanted it for him too. Yet, he had tried heroin and it was going to haunt him for the rest of his life. I couldn't get the lawyer's words out of my mind..."You can never trust him again now that he's tried heroin."

Chad arrived in Chicago to the first practice and ended up separating his shoulder the first time on the ice. When he told me, I pleaded with him to come home. He ended up losing the keys for his vehicle and was living in a motel with his best friend Dylan Martin, because the house they were supposed to be moving in had fallen through.

In October, they found a place to live in. Chad moved into a house in Chicago with a few friends. He still wanted to finish his schooling and he thought he'd have the best opportunity to do that down there. Even though his career with the junior hockey league was over, he played on one of the teams at the university: The Robert Morris University Eagles. He was doing his best to make things work.

He knew his dreams of playing professional hockey were over. However, he wanted to be in the hockey world as business man. He dreamed of managing and owning an NHL hockey team. Chad and Dylan started taking sports business classes with the goal of owning their own team. Chad always had amazing leadership skills and was motivated to make something for himself and support his family.

I talked to his coach every so often and he said that Chad had been doing well in school and was in a great training routine. He told me Chad was getting in good shape, that his relationship with Jamie was strong, and things were looking up. I wanted to believe the good news. I honestly hoped that things would stay good.

Unfortunately, that didn't last long. Chad got a kidney infection. By the time he got to the hospital he was extremely sick. He should have gone much earlier, but being the strong kid he's always been, he waited.

He called me from the hospital to tell me what happened. I told him I'd come down to meet with him. I just had to find someone to cover my shifts at work.

"No, it's okay, mom," he said. "Don't worry. Dylan is here with me."

Dylan was his best friend and roommate.

"Dylan's going to stay overnight with me," he added.

"But you're gonna love this, Mom," he was laughing. "They asked me who my next of kin was and I told them Dylan was – I told them he was my gay best friend."

Even with a debilitating kidney infection, he still had a strong enough sense of humor to mess with the nursing staff and his best friend (neither Chad or Dylan are gay).

I had to laugh.

"Chad, I need to talk to the nurses. You can't have any pain medication, because once you're addicted to Vicodin and a known heroin user, you can't have any sort of pain medication again. Not even once. Put the nurses on the phone. Let me talk to them," I said to him.

"I already told them, Mom," he said. "It's under control."

I tried to get him to put them on the phone, but he insisted it was already taken care of.

I called the hospital back to speak directly to the nurses, but, since he'd jokingly named Dylan as his "next of kin" they weren't able to discuss specifics with me about whether or not Chad had been put on pain medication. I was furious. What started as a simple joke was now keeping me from getting vital information about my son. I explained his history as best as I could, but they wouldn't really tell me anything. I told them he is not going to admit to you that he has an addiction issue because he is proud and he doesn't want to have it.

I made plans to drive down there and see him myself, but by the time I was ready to leave he'd been released from the hospital. My parents told me they'd keep an eye on him. They were retired and didn't have work commitments like I did, so they left to go visit him.

Chad recovered quickly and was able to get back on the ice quickly. He seemed to be getting better. To be finding himself. I honestly felt like things were starting to go his way, that things were on the way up.

***

Two days later, on November 19th, 2014, I went out for a run with my friend Kim. I didn't know it that morning, but this would become the defining day of my life.

Kim was one of the few people that I had really confided in about all the struggles Chad had been going through and how I'd been dealing with them. As we were jogging, we were chatting about how awesome Chad was doing and how my parents had just been down there to see him. I felt so optimistic and happy, like everything was going to turn out okay.

That night I went to the local hockey game and then headed to my new boyfriend's house, Jason Zahara. It was a beautiful night. Clear and crisp, perfect for hanging in the hot tub. The stars were exceptionally clear. The two of us were taking it all in and enjoying a glass of wine, when all of the sudden my dad came around the corner and walked into the back yard.

"Erin," he said. "You need to come with me right now."

I was completely surprised to see my dad at that hour and in my boyfriend's backyard. "What's wrong, Dad?" I asked.

"It's Chad," he replied.

"What happened to Chad?" I could feel the terror leaking into my voice as I asked.

"You need to come with me right now."

I leaped out of the hot tub, threw on a hoodie and hopped in the car. Honestly, I don't even know if I was wearing pants.

When we got home my dad said, "There's someone that needs to talk to you."

My mom was on the phone and I could see Kaeley was pacing back and forth. The look in her eyes was pure fear. My mom immediately handed me the phone.

"Hello?" I said.

"Are you Erin Miller?" a man asked. His tone was serious.

"Yes."

"My name is Dr. Hall. Are you Chad Miller's mom?" he asked.

"Yes, I am...Why?"

"You need to come to Chicago as soon as you can, Ms. Miller," he answered. "Chad was brought in here today. We had to put him on life support and we needed to wait until we talked to you...you are his next of kin, right?"

"What?!" I almost screamed into the phone. I felt like I'd been stabbed in the heart. "What is happening?" I pleaded. "Let me talk to him."

"He can't speak. He is on life support. He was at his home and was brought in by ambulance. They suspect it was an overdose and that he might have choked on his own vomit. We don't know for sure just yet."

In that one moment, everything in my world came crashing down.

Chapter 10

Because I worked in a hospital, I knew exactly what was going on behind the scenes. I'd seen this same thing happen to others a thousand times. I was horrified that this was now our reality. How could this happen to my own son?

Tears were welling up in my eyes. Mom, dad, and Kaeley were staring at me.

"Erin, you need to get there," someone said. It was all a blur. I couldn't think straight.

I called Ryan, Chad's step-father, right away.

"Ryan, we need to get to Chicago as fast as we can. There's been an accident with Chad."

It was 11pm. There were no flights until tomorrow, so we hopped in the car and just started driving. Chicago is a 15 hour drive from

Portage la Prairie. My mom called every airport on the way down there to see if there were any flights to get us there faster.

I kept my phone glued to me so the doctors could get a hold of me. The entire drive down my phone didn't stop ringing. It was phone call after phone call from Chad's friends, coaches, and his girlfriend.

The doctors kept calling me. They needed to get permission from me to immediately put him on dialysis because his kidneys were failing. He needed surgery, catheters, and feeding tubes. It was a complete disaster. Before the doctor called me, he had got the history about Chad and I could hear his empathy and compassion. It was breaking his heart to be seeing what he was seeing while talking to me . I was freaking out.

My mom was able to find us a flight out of Grand Forks, North Dakota, connecting in Minneapolis and then on to Chicago. We boarded the plane and got settled in to take off when all of the sudden the captain made an announcement. The flight was going to be delayed by an hour. That meant we were going to miss our connecting flight.

I nearly lost it.

I begged the flight crew to hurry and do everything they could, that my son was in the hospital and I had to get to him.

They said, "I'm sorry, we can't."

I felt completely out of control. I needed to get to Chicago.

Grand Forks is tiny and there are only a few flights a day that leave from there. With every minute we sat there on the tarmac I felt my life falling apart. It was the worst feeling knowing that my son was dying and I could do nothing about it. I had to get to Chad. "Please do not let him die," I prayed, but it was more like a plea of desperation. My heart was breaking.

When we finally made it to Chicago, it was a mad rush to get to Chad. I will never forget walking into the hospital. Even with all my hospital experience, I could never have prepared myself for this.

I walked into the room and saw my beautiful boy laying on the bed with tubes in his body and assisting him to breathe. The life support machine clicked and hissed as it pumped air into his lungs. His arm was wrapped up in bandages. There were doctors and nurses working all around him. Flashes of him as a newborn baby popped into my mind as I looked at him. I collapsed on the ground and began to sob.

The nurses helped me get over to Chad's bedside and I took hold of his hand as I tried my best to embrace him without disturbing all of the life support devices. Tears streamed down my face. My body racked with full body sobs. It was my worst nightmare.

A few minutes later, a group of doctors came in and took us over to the family room. The doctors started spouting off their best guesses about what they believed had happened and what the plan of action was from here. They told me he would remain on life support while they worked to do their best to help him.

I spent the next three days sitting by Chad's bedside, holding his hands, saying prayers, begging him to come back. I only left his side to go to the bathroom or to pray in the chapel.

I was not a religious person. In fact, up until that point I'd never really prayed to God for anything, but Chad needed it. I needed it. We all needed divine intervention.

So, every day I would sit in that chapel for 20 minutes and pray for a miracle – anything – to happen. I hoped that he would just get up and walk, that he would no longer have to be on life support. Or at the very least I could get him home to Portage la Prairie.

Friends, family, and coaches were constantly in and out of the hospital to check on him and give us support. Ryan, my ex-husband, came down. I'll never forget the look on his face when he first saw Chad. He was a tough guy, but his heart was broken. I'd never seen him so sad or distraught.

By day four our hope was running thin. Chad started looking tired, like his body was shutting down. I felt like any chance of a miracle was running out. I hadn't eaten anything for four days, but somehow, I was still throwing up constantly. I was sick with fear. My mom tried her best to support me and be there for me, but what could she really do?

On the fifth day, something changed in me. The doctors and nurses were all working on Chad. I felt completely powerless and out of control. I just wanted him to get better. And then something came over me. I remember standing up on a chair in the room.

"I'm stepping out of being a bystander right now," I said firmly. "Today I am pretending that this is me laying in the bed and I am Chad. What would I want Chad to decide for me?" This way I knew I could never regret the decisions I had to make.

I had spent days praying for a miracle, feeling helpless to do anything. I needed to step in and make decisions now as his mom and what was best for him and the family. I had to accept the fact that it was unlikely after 5 days that he was going to survive.

Word of Chad's circumstances had started to spread. By this time "Miller Strong" was trending around the world for Chad, sending prayer and support to all of us in the hospital room to keep "Miller Strong."

So I began to do what I could to make arrangements. I called the McKenzie funeral chapel back in Portage la Prairie. The nurses started prepping me to take him off life support. I had to make decisions about him being a donor. And then, there was a real logistical issue. Chad was a Canadian boy who had overdosed and would likely die on American soil. How were we going to get him back to Canada? How do we take him through immigration to be buried back at home?

It was gut wrenching decision after gut wrenching decision. It was almost too much to handle. The only way I could get through it was to tell myself that I can't make decisions as his mom right now. I have to make decisions as if I were Chad trying to look after his mother in this horrific situation. And that's what I did. I kept asking myself, "Okay, what would Chad want you to do now?" And then the answers would come. Of course, he would be a donor. Of course, he would want to be buried back in Canada. Decision after decision, this was my process.

The police came and saw me in the hospital. They had all his personal belongings, computer, phone, wallet, school books, journal, his black adidas backpack, everything. Because his case was suspected drug use, they needed to evaluate the incident and his belongings. They were treating the case as a drug induced homicide. This is when I found out who sold Chad the drugs. I was horrified.

The police weren't 100 percent sure exactly how he overdosed, and I didn't know either. As his mother, I couldn't understand how he could have even gotten access to these drugs. Chad didn't even have any money. I asked one of the officers, "How does this even happen? Chad's a student with almost no money. How could he even afford something like heroin?"

The officer replied, "Erin, he could go outside of the school and get this stuff for $10."

I was shocked.

$10 for a deadly addiction that could kill. The thought of it made me want to scream.

The Chicago Police explained to me that Chicago was in a drug epidemic and in 5 years heroin would be killing my son's friends as well. We all stood around Chad's bed and held hands and prayed that one day I would be his voice – doctors, nurses, police , friends, family, spiritual care – we all prayed that this was happening to Chad for a bigger purpose.

After 9 days on life support, I had to make the hardest decision of my life. Chad was deteriorating every day. The nurses and doctors were doing everything they could, but I had to face the fact…

Chad was not coming back. He was brain dead.

I had to make the decision to take him off of life support. It was the worst day of my entire life.

I signed the papers to authorize removing him from life support. I gave him a bath beforehand, so his body would be clean. I picked out the clothes I wanted him to wear on his way back to Canada. I had all the paper work done.

Kaeley designed and ordered the Miller Strong /Hang Loose bracelets that we would be handing out at his funeral. I called Jason, Chad's biological father, and told him what had happened and that I wanted him to say whatever he wanted to Chad. He needed to say "goodbye." I put him on speaker phone and I listened to a father say goodbye to a son he never even knew. It was heartbreaking.

Later, when I sat alone with Chad, I remember telling Chad every single thing I ever wanted to tell him. How much I loved him. How honored I was to be his mother. I told him I would be okay and that he would be okay too. I laid beside him and we listened to Taylor Swift songs. She was his favorite artist. We watched the Pittsburgh Penguins game – Sidney Crosby was his favorite player. I would never let anyone forget him and I would never forget him. He was my Clun (that was my nickname for him), my life , my purpose and my hero.

I sat by his side, holding his hand as they removed all the apparatuses that were keeping him alive. We didn't know exactly what to expect. The specialist said, "Sometimes people pass right away once they're removed from life support, some people continue on their own for a while."

Chad was blessed with holy water and prayer from his friends' parents that had taken a special liking to him.

With classic Chad Miller toughness, he seemed to be hanging on tight. He breathed on his own for the next 2 days. They moved us from ICU to palliative care.

As we left ICU, the girl coming to take over Chad's room was a 17-year-old hockey player that had been hit into the boards and had internal damage to her organs. When I heard her story, I thought, "Chad could be her donor." It seemed fitting to have Chad pass a part of himself to a fellow hockey player in need. And that's exactly what he was able to do. He was able to help save someone else.

In the Palliative Care Unit, Chad lay there brain dead and breathing on his own. At 2:30pm that afternoon, his breathing changed in a single breath. I ran and got the nurse. Sure enough, they said, he's transitioning. Everyone took their turn to say goodbye to him. I took the last turn.

As I held Chad's hand, I remember telling him, "I promise that I'm going to be okay. I promise that you are going to be okay. This is not your fault. I know this is not what you wanted. I'm going to make sure people never forget you, that they know your story. I love you, Chad."

When he was a baby, I always sang to him the song *You Are My Sunshine*. I began to sing...

"You are my Sunshine, my only Sunshine, you make me happy when skies are gray. You'll never know, Dear, how much I love you, so please don't take my Sunshine away..."

I put my hands on his chest and I told him, "You can go now, Clun. You're safe. I love you."

It was like he was waiting for me to tell him that it was okay to go to the other side. And I felt him take in one last breath in and then his whole body relaxed.

I kissed him on his lips and held his head in my arms.

And then he was gone.

Chapter 11

A part of me died that day with Chad. When he let out that final exhale my heart broke into a thousand pieces. I wept and wept, waves of sobbing taking over my body. And I instantly regretted signing that fucking paper to pull him off life support. That would haunt me for years.

We all got into the vehicle and started the long drive back to Canada. Chad had more friends than all of us combined, so the whole drive back people were reaching out to us from all over the world to offer their condolences and support.

The next few days were a blur to me. I hardly remember anything. I felt like a zombie walking through life. I just wanted my son to come back and be with me. But there was nothing I could do, and that was the worst feeling in the world.

Chad's body had to stay in the States for the time being, so they could prepare him to come back home. The first few days of being back in Portage, my house looked like a flower shop. There were flowers covering nearly every available surface in the house from all of the people that knew and loved Chad and our family. There were streams of people coming over to the house, bringing us food, wanting to talk to us. It was overwhelming and beautiful to have that much outpouring of love and support.

Everyone was asking me when the funeral was going to be and where it would be held. I was in such a broken state that I didn't even want to have a funeral. I outright refused to have one at first. I did not want to attend my own son's funeral. No mother should have to bury their child. I guess it was my own way of trying to avoid the inevitable.

But it was almost like Chad spoke to me. A thought came to me, "What would Chad want?" And I realized that, yes, of course he would want a funeral. He would want his friends, family, the community to be able to come and say their goodbyes to him so that they could have closure. So we went ahead with it.

No one tells you that when a loved one dies that you're going to have to make decisions about what they wear to their funeral. It's a big deal. It's the last outfit that you or anyone else will ever see them in again. I'd picked out hundreds of outfits for Chad over his life. None of them were as difficult as this decision.

Then there were the logistical and financial questions. How are we going to pay for Chad's funeral? How are we going to get him through Immigration back into Canada? Where are we going to have the funeral?

A lot of my friends wanted me to have the funeral at the hockey arena since that was where Chad was in his element. It didn't sit well with me. I had too many memories there, and Kaeley was going to be in a hockey tournament playing a game there the weekend after the funeral. It felt wrong to me. I knew it had to be at a church.

The day of the funeral, December 12, 2014, was a blur for me. I hardly remember it the emotions were so overwhelming. I do remember that the church was absolutely packed. I walked into the church as a mother that lost her child to a drug overdose. My brother delivered a beautiful eulogy for him. Kaeley recited a poem she'd written for Chad. I sat in the front row in complete disbelief that all of this was happening. I tried to be strong for Kaeley and for the community, but inside I was broken.

***

In the weeks and months following the funeral, the grief had taken complete hold of me. To make matters worse, it was Christmas time. I didn't care about anything. I walked around in a daze. The only thing that kept me here was my beautiful daughter Kaeley. She was the only reason that I had to live.

I would wake up almost every night from horrible nightmares, laying in a pool of my own sweat. I didn't sleep for more than an hour at a time for months. I don't know how, but someone had gotten ahold of my doctor. I went to go see him and he gave me medication to help me sleep.

During my waking hours, it was all I could do to get to work. I needed anything that could distract me from my grief. It got so bad that I agreed to go see a grief counselor.

When I showed up for my first session, I walked into her office and sat down. She looked at me in very strange way. Her eyes looked down at my feet.

"Where are your shoes?" she asked.

I looked down at my feet. I was barefoot. And it was winter in Canada.

I honestly didn't know how I'd gotten there without shoes. I didn't even notice I wasn't wearing them. That's how bad my grief was. It was making me forget the simplest things. I just wanted my baby boy back.

***

My debilitating grief was unfair to Kaeley. She had lost so much. She'd lost everything that was normal to her. She'd lost her brother tragically, and now, even though I was still physically there, she'd lost her mother in a sense too. I know it was horrible for her. I was just trying to do the best that I could every day to try and get a little bit better for her.

It was around this time that I got a call from Jamie, Chad's girlfriend. I couldn't believe it, but she was pregnant with Chad's child. She'd gotten pregnant before Chad overdosed. I was going to be a Grandma. I was overwhelmed with emotion when she told me the news. Jamie was far enough along in her pregnancy before she told me and she revealed that her baby would be a boy also. I couldn't believe this. I just had an added addition to my family and the memory of Chad.

My grandson, Keaton Crosby Miller, was born on Father's Day that year. Jamie asked me to choose his middle name. I felt the name Crosby was fitting as Sydney Crosby, a famous NHL player, was a hero of Chad's. While I was elated to learn of Jamie's pregnancy, it didn't come without some emotional pain over how this sweet boy would come into the world and never know his Dad. Since Jamie was American and Chad was Canadian, it was a long process to get Keaton to become a dual citizen and eventually they both moved to Canada.

By the spring of 2015, I was starting to improve a little bit. Maybe it was the warmth after that brutal winter, but I committed to being there for my daughter Kaeley. I still had a very long way to go in overcoming my grief, but I would do my best to support her.

Kaeley was doing a lot of amazing things. She was running for student council and became the president of the high school. She was playing sports and keeping herself active. I was so proud of her and I loved watching her in her element. She was the captain of the high school hockey team.

Just when I thought I was making progress, the nightmares came back with a vengeance. It was like I was experiencing my own version of post-traumatic stress disorder. I would see someone that reminded me of Chad and I would get massively triggered, having full emotional breakdowns. I was disassociating nonstop, living in complete terror. In hindsight, continuing to work in the hospital was probably the worst thing that I could have done. Being around that many traumatic incidents so regularly was not helping my recovery. I decided I needed to get psychological help to get things under control.

Chapter 12

I starting seeing a psychiatrist. She helped me start to get my nightmares under control so I could at least sleep a little. I also began working with Jane, a Cognitive Behavioral Therapist (CBT) who helped me over the next year. She was a tiny woman who wore reading glasses and very nice dresses. She made me feel welcome and had a lot of compassion and empathy for me.

During one of my sessions with Jane, she asked me what my values were. I remember sitting there and I couldn't come up with a single value I stood for. I felt guilty. I felt ashamed. I had survival guilt that I was alive while my son was not. I felt like I was a terrible mother and that all of this had happened because of me. I started believing that this was 100% my fault.

My PTSD was being triggered by everything around me and I couldn't keep anything straight.

It was debilitating to live with the pain of loss and then the pain of "what ifs."

What if I'd only checked in on him more? What if I had died instead of him? What if I could've saved him? What if I didn't let him go back to Chicago? Why did I sign the paper saying I was okay taking him off life support?

People would tell me how they had to put their cat or dog down and it was sick for me to think I had done the same thing to my child.

My thoughts were a train wreck and it was all I could do to get some semblance of control over them. It's like I was constantly fighting myself, all day, every day.

I did not know I had so much childhood trauma until Jane from CBT suggested I go to EMDR that the CBT was all she could do and EMDR would help

To top it all off, I realized that I had never really dealt with any of my own childhood trauma. I was still carrying around the burden of being sexually abused at 14, becoming a teenage mom and having an abortion.

EMDR Eye Movement desensitization and reprocessing helped me start to work through some of these things. I felt my brain start to open up, like a big blockage had all of the sudden become unplugged.

EMDR is an interactive psychological technique used to relieve stress. He took me back to my childhood and this is where I realized as an adult just how horrific my childhood was. Some sessions I felt I had progressed while other times I felt like nothing was happening. I was able to decrease emotional stress from my memory. He used to tell me to open up the lid in the box and put the thoughts in the box that I was no longer needing.

He also suggested that I try medical marijuana. Unfortunately, my psychiatrist didn't believe in the benefits of marijuana, so I could not get a medical card. I felt it would help me though, so I started using marijuana and CDB oils. I started being able to cope. It helped me slow down my mind and begin to finally sleep again.

I went to EMDR for a year and a half. He assured me that my symptoms and behaviors were directly related to all the trauma I had had throughout my life. Once I realized that a lot of my feelings, behaviors and thoughts were not only coming from grief, but my past, I started to be able to think more clearly.

The psychiatrist I was seeing, had put me on lots of medications at that point. I had a pill pack and I was spending a large portion of my paychecks on my medications. It was creating an incredible amount of horrific side effects. At night, my legs would cramp up so bad that it kept me from sleeping. My mind was foggy and confused on the medication. Then they'd change my medication and something else would happen to my body. I was on 12 medications at one point. It was horrible.

Around that time, I started to go to Dialectical Behavior Therapy. They recommended it to me because they said it would help me break my negative thought patterns and begin to find something that was positive in my life. The class was a group therapy class and I met a bunch of other amazing women who all came from completely different backgrounds than I did, but they were all going through their own version of hell. I never knew why each one of them was there I just knew they were all trying to put their lives back in order. They started to inspire me to take back control of my own life. It was actually kind of refreshing to not feel so alone. It felt comforting to know there were other women struggling as much as I was.

As I listened to the stories these women shared, I started to learn from them. Our stories resonated, and I could see myself in their shoes. As they worked through things, I worked through things. That's the power of having a tribe of people that are going through challenging things at the same time as you. Because it allows you to get a perspective you can't get when you're in survival mode, trying to protect your feelings from people that you know cannot relate nor understand you.

That's why I strongly encourage anyone who is suffering with trauma, pain, or difficult situations to find a community that can properly support them and they can support others. That's part of why we created the Miller Strong #17 Foundation. We wanted to build a community of people that could take a stand for the injustices in the world and create a safe haven for those that are suffering through pain and trauma. You can find out more details on our website at www.millerstrong17.com

***

Even though my mind was getting healthier and clearer from the support group, my body was deteriorating at an incredibly alarming rate. It felt like it was shutting down. My legs were hardly functioning and they were in constant pain. My diaphragm was closing. My body had bruises all over it because I was so iron deficient. I hadn't had my period in forever. I had ballooned up to over 200 pounds. I was peeing my pants, my bowels stopped working, and my hair was falling out. I had lumps under my armpits and breasts. My blood pressure was all over the map.

I also started to experience chronic pain in my lower back that ran up and down my right leg. At one point, I could barely stand. I did some research online and found out that it might be my sciatic nerve. I found out that an option for treatment was to see a chiropractor. I had never been to a chiropractor before so I was a bit scared.

A few months earlier, I had met a chiropractor named Dr. Sarlas at the Hospital Gala Dinner in town, so I decided to go see him. While I waited for him to see me, the receptionist handed me a questionnaire asking if I had any of the ailments they listed before our spoke with Dr. Sarlas. On a list of over a dozen problems, I had every single one of them. It made me sick.

When I saw Dr. Sarlas, I told him that I was there for my leg pain. I thought maybe if I didn't tell him that I had all of the problems on the list that they'd somehow go away. I explained the symptoms of the physical pain in my legs, and he looked at me and asked, "Is there any way you could be in emotional pain?"

I immediately started crying when he asked.

I had been walking around town thinking everyone knew what had happened to Chad and what a wreck I was. Yet, here was this man who didn't know. And there was something so refreshing about someone NOT knowing about my problems.

That's the challenge with physical and emotional trauma. It wraps your whole world up in it so you think everyone is as absorbed in it as much as you are. The reality is, they're thinking about their own lives. I was fighting the reality of Chad's passing and living in complete fear. I was still living the nightmare when others had moved on.

"I do have emotional pain," I said, after I stopped crying. "My son passed away." I told him everything.

When I finished speaking, Dr. Sarlas had tears coming down his eyes.

"I can release some of your emotional pain," he said. "But there are some side effects that could happen to you."

He said it was possible for me to have what he described to me as a seizure. Yet, the medications were already causing me inordinate amounts of trouble, so I figured it was worth the risk. I agreed. I was out of options

He went to work. He made a few adjustments on my body. I heard a few clicks. And then it was like a wave came over me. I remember not being able to see straight.

"Are you okay?" he asked.

"No, I'm not okay." I could barely get the words out.

I felt my whole body going unsteady. I could feel my body begin to release. It started to have little spasms, like the stuck energy inside of me was shaking itself out.

"This can happen," he said, trying to keep me calm. He'd told me before that it was a possibility.

I shouldn't have, but I took myself home. When I got home, I was drenched in sweat. I took all of my clothes off. My body temperature was rapidly rising. No matter what I did that night I could not get comfortable or cool. It felt like my body was bouncing all over the place, twitching, spasming, and shaking. I called Dr. Sarlas the next day and he asked me to come back.

This time, I brought my mom with me. Dr. Sarlas checked me out and said everything was releasing normally. He adjusted me a few more times, and then, unexpectedly, my body went into what I describe as a seizure. It was bouncing and shaking all over the place. My mom got scared and tried to hold me to comfort me, and I remember screaming at her, "Get your fucking hands off of me!"

It was so painful. I couldn't handle being touched as my body seized up. I tried walking and I could not walk straight.

"When is the last time you ate?" Dr. Sarlas asked.

"I don't know," I replied. My teeth chattered.

"When is the last time you had water?" he asked.

"I have no clue," I stammered.

There was so much energy contained in my body. I realized I had been living in this survival mode for years since Chad passed. I didn't want to look at myself or take care of myself, but it was starting to break. Waves of physical and emotional pain were being released from my body.

My parents had to take me to their house to stay with them, so I could have someone look after me for a few days. I tried to sleep, but my body kept twitching and jerking. It felt like energy was just oozing out of my body.

The next day I had to go back to the chiropractor again because the spasms still hadn't stopped. My friend Lynn took me. At this point, I could hardly walk. She had to hold my arm as we walked into the office and into the Dr.'s room. I felt like I was walking sideways, in a state of vertigo. When Dr. Sarlas saw me, he said, "You need to go to the emergency room now. You need IV fluids and something to make your body rest."

My heart dropped. That was the last place I wanted to go to. I had just quit my job at the hospital to focus on my health. There was no way in hell I wanted to go back there.

"Erin, you have to go. Your body is in shock. It's like you took a deep breath in 4 years ago and you haven't exhaled since. You have to go there now." He wasn't kidding.

At the hospital, I had to use a wheelchair. I fell getting into the bed. My blood pressure and heart rate were through the roof. I thought I was going to die. My body finally calmed down once they gave me medication to help me sleep for a little while. After doing a little bit of bloodwork, they sent me home.

But the next day nothing was improved. My body was still spasming. I called my chiropractor again and he said, "Erin, you've got to go back to the hospital."

At the hospital, my blood pressure was back up. Once again, I felt like I was going to die. I had no control of my body. It felt like it was ejecting every last bit of energy it had.

At that time, because of my intense grief from Chad's passing, there were concerns that I was mentally ill. The physical release from the work with the chiropractor made it laser clear to me that while my body was having all sorts of ailments, my mind was clearer than ever. I knew what was going on and that my body was doing everything it could to release the trauma that had been stored in it. In fact, I hadn't felt that mentally clear for a long time.

I was finally getting some relief and rest when the physiatrist walked in. She explained to me she had been consulted by the health care team to come and do an urgent psychiatric assessment. I was shocked. I was finally resting and now I had to explain why I was in the emergency room.

The psychiatrist was with a resident doctor. I started explaining everything that had happened the past couple days. She told me that the chiropractor was adding to my issues and forbade me from going back to see him. I tried to explain how his work was releasing the stored emotional trauma in me. She wouldn't listen to me. I was told I had to go on an anti-psychotic medication or she would "Form 4" me under the Mental Health Act and the police would be coming to detain me and take me to a psychiatric hospital. I pleaded with her to call Dr.

Sarlas to explain the situation. I assured her I was of clear mind, but it was my body that was releasing.

Reluctantly, I agreed to go on the medication and not to go back to Dr. Sarlas. I was discharged.

While the energetic release of all of that trauma from my body was painful, it made me acutely aware of one thing:

I needed to take time to heal.

My family and I decided that I did not need the medication the physiatrist required me to take. Instead, we believed it was best for me to get off all of the medications that were creating these problems in the first place and start to take control back of my life. I continued going to see Dr. Sarlas and started going to a personal trainer to get my body back into shape.

I decided that the best way for me to heal was to get out of Portage la Prairie. There were too many memories there.

Chapter 13

About 4 months before I had the seizure in Dr. Sarla's chiropractic office, I ran into a man who made a big impact on me. I was at work at the hospital one day when we bumped into each other. I had known him in the community for a long time. His name was Ben Maendel, a Hutterite man and minister. I was so sick he didn't recognize me at first. I told him, "I don't even recognize myself anymore, Ben."

I couldn't drive anymore. I wasn't allowed to pick up my grandson from daycare. My volunteers were basically running the hospital foundation. My hair was falling out and I couldn't control my bladder at times. I couldn't even take in deep breathes it was so painful.

"You should come visit me and Mary sometime, Erin," he said. Mary was his wife.

I had been to Baker Community where they lived several times before. They were an extension of my family. It was a beautiful place, surrounded by incredible nature.

The next day I went to see him and Mary. We had an incredible conversation. Real, authentic, vulnerable, and loving. It was so opposite from what I'd get in town with most people questioning my sanity.

At their house, Ben told me, "It's going to be okay. You can let go of what you've been holding on to."

I felt my soul relax a little.

"When was the last time you prayed, Erin?" he asked.

"I don't know. It's been a while. I remember praying in the hospital asking God to save Chad and bring us a miracle," I replied.

"Do you think it might be time you try again, Erin?"

Even though a part of me wanted to resist what he was saying, another part of me knew it was right. My life was LITERALLY not working. I was losing in almost every area of my life. It felt like I was dying.

So I went home. I took my dog Finn, I grabbed Chad's journal and I dragged myself into Chad's bedroom. I had his journal in one hand and a hand written note in the other. The note said something along the lines of 'if God wants me to die then that's what I'm okay with too.' I had my dog because I knew that my boyfriend would come looking for us and that my family couldn't survive finding me dead.

As I laid on the floor, I started praying. I prayed to God that I was sorry for every single thing that I could have done better in my life. I acknowledged that had I known differently at certain times in my life, I would have done better for my children. In my prayers, I forgave every single person that had done me or my kids wrong. I asked God if there was a bigger purpose to why Chad died and I prayed he tell me what it was. I felt completely at the end of my rope. Despite all of my options I was losing in my life. There was nowhere for me to go except to surrender my life to God or die.

So, I prayed that I would know what needed to happen and that I'd accept whatever the outcome was. I closed my eyes for what might have been five minutes.

And that's when it hit me: I had no purpose to live for.

As I sat in Chad's bedroom I decided to change that.

"Chad," I said. "I'm never going to forget you. I'm going to sell the house, quit my job, and I'm going to rewrite your story."

And in that moment, I faced one of my biggest fears.

Chapter 14

It was time to let the past go and move forward. It was time to finally face my fear of letting a piece of myself and my son move on. It was the scariest decision because of all of the memories wrapped around it, but I knew in my heart that I needed to sell my house.

Sitting there in Chad's room with all of those memories, my body completely broken, and my soul ready to find healing, I knew that it was the way forward.

I'd been talking about selling my house for a while, but it was too emotional for me to actually pull the trigger on it. I'd gone to see a realtor five times before and never moved forward. The idea of selling the home hurt me deeply. How could I let my son down like this? It always felt like it would be the last part of him that I was finally letting go of. I felt that in selling the home it was the final acknowledgement of my failure as his mother.

But that day, when I resolved to rewrite Chad's story, I knew it was the only way forward. Everyone else had already accepted that Chad had passed. They had come to their sense of peace and moved forward with their lives. I was the last one to do so. I didn't want to let go of my boy. I was also scared because I didn't even know myself. He was my identity from such a young age. I had to accept things

My realtor, Rhonda Lodwick, was very helpful. She was compassionate about what I was going through, and she quickly found a potential buyer who made an offer. The only problem was I didn't want to sell it to him.

He was a single man. I had raised my family in this home. We'd had so many kids' parties, barbecues, we even had a trampoline in the backyard. It was thick with family memories, and I wanted it to go to a family that would write their own stories on top of ours.

The night before it was supposed to close, I didn't know what to do, so I went outside in the cold, winter night and made a fire. It was one of our favorite things to do as a family. As I was sitting outside in the cold reminiscing about all the great times I texted Rhonda, my realtor, to say that I didn't want to sell the house to a single man. I explained I thought the house should go to a family. I looked up after sending the text and I noticed there was a man having a cigarette outside on my neighbors deck He approached the fence.

He looked up at me and said, "Erin? Are you Erin Miller?"

"Yes," I said.

"I'm Harold Clayton. I'm the guy that's going to be buying your house tomorrow," he said.

"Oh, that's funny," I replied. "Because I just texted my realtor and I decided I'm actually not going to sell it. It needs to go to a family. I'm sorry."

"Erin," he smiled and looked right into my eyes. "I know how hard it is going to be for you to sell your house."

"Yeah right," I thought.

He continued. "My son died of a drug overdose in 2011. I know how hard it is. I've had to do this before."

I was stunned.

He told me when he'd walked into Chad's room he could feel something. and he knew he needed to buy the house.

Chad's room wasn't staged for selling the house. It was exactly the way it was 4 years ago when my Uncle Brian had moved all of Chad's stuff back from Chicago.

I called Rhonda, my realtor, back the next morning to ask her about Harold.

"Did you tell him about Chad?" I asked.

"No," she said. "I didn't tell him anything. He just walked into Chad's room as I was showing him the home and it was like he was paralyzed when he got into that room. I saw tears start to come down his eyes. He held Chad's jersey in his hand for a while."

She told me Harold's wife had recently passed away and he was moving back to Portage la Prairie to be closer to his friends.

All my reservations about selling it to him melted away. We had too much in common. Of course, the house had to go to him. I agreed to sell.

Chapter 15

After that things seemed to really start working out for me. I felt this new sense of life and purpose. I was starting to believe in God again. I felt more supported in life than I ever had before.

I sold my house and moved to Winnipeg with money in my pocket. I decided I would take the next year off for me. I'd spent the last four years hiding, suppressing, trying to cope with life. I finally felt like it was time to break free from this cycle of fear and trauma and really live again. If someone suggested something new that I hadn't tried before (as long as it was ethical and moral of course), then my answer was usually, "I can't think of one reason why not?"

I started going to the gym, reading books, doing yoga, making new friends, started seeing a psychologist, doing Reiki, going to float tanks, being mindful, practicing meditation, and cooking again. Kaeley and I were starting our new life and did lots of self-care. I picked up some contract marketing work and started making plans for the future.

In January 2018, right after I sold my house, my former colleague and friend Dr. Michelle Bailes, suggested that I learn how to scuba dive. She said it's an amazing skill to have that can take you all over the world and will help you with your PTSD. Well, Manitoba isn't exactly near the ocean, but we do have a lot of lakes. So, I figured out where I could start to learn in a pool and then once I was certified I took it to the local lakes. It was bliss being under water. Everything was so still and quiet. I felt so at peace.

Dr. Bailes convinced me to go to Indonesia the following year to go diving with her. That way I'd have plenty of time to practice and get my gear sorted out locally. She would set me up with her friend Jackie when she got back from an upcoming diving trip to Indonesia.

Dr. Bailes flew off to Indonesia. While she was there she broke her leg and was brought back to Canada on March 18, 2018. Within 12 hours of being home, she died in the hospital because of a pulmonary embolism that had built up in her leg. My heart broke. I couldn't believe this had happened to my friend.

Learning how to scuba dive was the farthest thing from my mind now. I couldn't believe Michelle had gone like that. It was devastating and I could feel myself start to be pulled back towards that dark vortex I'd been in before.

Yet, something strange happened to me a few months later in July. The voice inside told me, "Erin, go get your scuba license. You know Michelle would want you to do this." It felt like someone was literally pushing me to go do it.

So I conceded. I started taking private scuba diving lessons. It was super difficult. I almost drowned a few times in the pool. It was terrible. It was a lot harder than I ever thought it would be. But every day I'd ask myself, "Is there any reason I'm not going to do this?" The only reason I could come up with was that I was scared because I almost drowned.

I didn't want to quit. I was determined to learn how to scuba dive. This was the first thing I was doing in my life for me and I knew it would help me get better and heal. I could already tell that it was. It was giving me something to focus on. I was learning a new skill. It was challenging me in a good way.

To get your open water PADI certification you have to do all the skills in open water which was in West Hawk lake near where I live in Winnipeg. I had to go pick up all my gear at the dive shop on the way to the lake. While in the shop, I asked if anyone knew my friend Michelle Bailes before I headed out to the Lake.

To my surprise, a girl named Jackie turned around and said, "I am Michelle's friend."

I started crying. I said, " You're Jackie! Dr. Bailes friend that was going to teach me how to dive…."

I told her I was here to learn to dive in honor of Michelle. She loved it. I told her a brief story of my life.

"Erin," she said. "I have all of Michelle's diving gear with me here. It's for sale. I could have sold it already but it wasn't to the right person."

I couldn't believe it. To me, it was another sign that God was guiding my path and that I was moving in the right direction.

I had to buy it. I wanted to dive in Michelle's gear.

I wouldn't let her tragic passing go by without honoring her memory.

Chapter 16

Once I learned to scuba dive, I committed to going to Gili Trawangan, an island in Indonesia. Before I left though, I wanted to make sure my family was looked after. It was time to take all of the pain of the past, the tragic loss of Chad, the memory of Dr. Michelle Bailes, of all the people that had been left behind in some way and focus my purpose on something that would leave a legacy behind. I decided it was time to start the foundation I'd been dreaming about.

The foundation would be called Miller Strong #17 Foundation in honor of my son Chad Miller. Both my kids wore number 17 as the captains of their high school hockey teams. The foundation's mission would be to make the world better, one person at a time.

Things started to fall in to place as I figured out the right team of people to help me create, launch, and administrate it. I started to get investors and support. Momentum was building.

It was amazing to feel this incredible sense of purpose knowing that I was creating something that would not only honor the legacy of my son but would re-write his story and use it for good for others.

I also wanted to use the foundation as a platform to be a voice for people that had experienced tragedies like my friend Lori McFarland. Her daughter, Amber McFarland, had been missing from our community for 10 years. She went missing on October 18, 2008 and no one had been able to find her. The police eventually declared her dead and her case became an unsolved murder. Yet, if there was any chance of hope that our foundation could help find her and be a voice for all of the other missing children in the country, then I wanted to do that. Nothing is more devastating than a parent losing a child to death, murder or abduction. It's horrible.

We decided to launch the foundation on October 18, 2018 on the 10-year anniversary of Amber McFarland's disappearance. We had months to prepare, so Lori and I decided to go on a girl's trip to California to celebrate and honour our children.

We were huge fans of the Ellen show and we thought, "What if we went and told her directly about what we're doing with the Miller Strong #17 Foundation?" It was worth a shot.

I brought my lucky, golden basket with me. It was made in Ghana and part of the proceeds went to help women's initiatives. Everywhere I went, people took photos with me and the basket. I figured it couldn't hurt to bring it along and help us out.

Right before we left for California, I got an unexpected phone call. Jason, Chad's biological father, reached out to me. He was in a horrible space. Addicted, neglecting his other children and his relationships, and destroying his life. He called me because he had lost his own "Chad's Band" and wanted a new one.

I met up with Jason to give him one and when I saw him I couldn't believe how horrible he looked. Jason was literally killing himself with his drug and alcohol addictions. I gave him the wrist band and then the real reason he wanted to meet with me came out. Jason asked me for money to get his license back. They'd taken it and his car from him because of his addictions.

I remember going to talk to Jason's friend, and she went on and on about how neglectful he was being as a father. It was hurting me to know that Chad's half-brothers and sisters were having to experience this. I knew Jason needed help. I'd been given help when I didn't expect it. It was time for me to put my faith to the test and do the same for him.

I called a rehab center that was close by and asked about the process of getting help. I also asked how much it would cost to get Jason help. It was not a small amount - over $20,000. I took a deep breath, but I knew what I had to do.

I went back to meet with Jason.

"I'm not going to give you the money to get your license and car back. But I am going to help you," I said to him.

I leaned in and told him the hard truth he needed to hear. "You need to go to Rehab. You're not showing up good for anyone, including yourself. You need help."

I took him to the Rehab center and paid for his treatment.

It was one of the hardest moments of my life to give grace to the man that had physically threatened me and abandoned my son.

But I guess that's what forgiveness is about; giving something to someone when they deserve it the least.

Now I was ready to go full steam ahead on my own journey of healing. I left for the States with Lori and our plans to launch the Foundation.

We had an amazing time in California. While we didn't get to meet Ellen personally, there were so many examples of God working in my life and guiding me to follow my intuition to build the foundation. One of the most powerful examples was a church we went to that had been recommended to us by a man I sat next to on the flight from Vancouver to San Francisco . The church was called Hillsong. We'd never heard of it, but it's become a huge global movement.

When we got to the church we were waiting in line to enter the service and a girl came up to me and handed me a bracelet. The bracelet had written on it, "Be the energy you want to attract." I loved it. It set the tone for what was to come.

Before Chad's passing, my daughter Kaeley and I started making wrist bands in honor of Chad. We called them #chadsbands. They had the words "Hang Loose" inscribed on them. Chad always would pose with the Hawaiian Shaka sign that surfers use to say, "Hang Loose."

I gave the girl a Chad's Band and I put the bracelet she'd given me on my wrist and walked into the church. The church was incredible. It kind of felt like Disney World. There were thousands of people in the church. The energy was through the roof. There were so many bodies and the energy was contagious. I saw the stage and it looked like we were getting ready for a concert not church.

We stood in line for security and they all took notice of my basket. I laugh because I had a knife in my basket that I'd forgotten about. We had a picnic the day before and brought the knife to cut up limes for our Corona. I loved that they listened to why I had this and there was zero judgment. They were really excited that we were from Canada and there to take in the service.

We found our seats and after a little while I turned to Lori and said, "I'm going to go get us a coffee."

I went to the coffee station and paid for our drinks. And then something strange happened.

It was almost as if time slowed down. Even though I had been slowly opening up my mind and heart to God, it was still a very new journey for me. I felt mostly like a Christian, but maybe I was scared to call myself that or put my faith in a higher power after so much tragedy in my life. I felt like I was 99.99% of the way there to committing to my faith, but there was that 0.01% left until I was all in.

As that time distortion came over me, a thought entered my mind: "I'm going to leave my credit card on the coffee counter. If it comes back to me before the end of the service, I will be all in."

I took the coffees, left the card at the coffee station and walked away. I went back to where our seats were and told Lori what I had done.

"Erin Miller!" she said firmly. "Go back and get that credit card right now! You're crazy!"

"I'm not crazy," I replied with complete calm. "Either that card comes back to me or it doesn't."

We continued watching the service. The pastor was talking about the labels that people put on themselves and others. He talked about how we put on the labels of guilt, shame, and all of these bad things about us and others. I felt like he was speaking right to me. I'd piled so many layers of those labels on myself over my life.

The pastor then began to talk about replacing those labels with happiness, with love, with God, with gratitude, with forgiveness. I felt lighter, like a weight had been lifted off of my shoulders.

A few minutes later, a guy came up and taped me on the shoulder.

"Erin? Are you Erin Miller?" he asked.

"Yes," I replied, confused.

"Here's your credit card," he said as he handed it to me. "I found it at the coffee station. I didn't know if it was from this service or last night's. I called your credit card company to see when the last time you used it was and it was a taxi to get here, so I knew you were here, somewhere."

Holy shit. I couldn't believe it. It really happened.

A moment later, Brandon, the pastor on stage asked, "Who wants to become a Christian today?"

I knew. I was all in. I raised my hand and walked up on stage. It was time to cement my faith.

Chapter 17

The launch party was scheduled for October 18, 2018. I was so excited leading up to it. The team was working to get everything together for the event. It was to be held it at the local community club Koko Platz Community Center in Portage la Prairie. It was the same spot where Chad had cut his chops and developed as a hockey player. I thought it was fitting.

The days leading up to the event the weather was unseasonably cold for October. It was -5 Celsius (nearly 20 degrees Fahrenheit). I remember praying that the weather would get nicer for the day of the party. We were going to have all of the festivities and tents set up outside. I didn't want the poor weather to affect the turnout.

The plan was for me to speak about Chad at the community center, and for Lori to hold a 10-year vigil for her daughter Amber in a different location in Portage. We were two Mom's taking a stand. We would talk at the same time but share a different yet similar story with hopes we would catch people's attention.

Brain Nelson, the pastor that I had sat beside on the plane to California, came and surprised Lori and I with his support. He brought a personalized prayer card for each of us that was made from the youth at Silicon Valley. It was magical.

Well, my prayers were answered. On the 18th, the weather was beautiful and warm. It was going to be an incredible day. Before the launch party, we had a get together at my parent's house with about 50 people. We were celebrating and drinking champagne. It was all about Chad. I couldn't stop smiling. The energy and joy in that house was unbelievable.

Just before we left to go to the Foundation launch party, I pulled my mom aside. I handed her a letter that I had written years before. In my deepest moments of pain over the loss of Chad, I had wanted to end my own life. I placed the suicide letter I had written in my mom's hand and I said, "You can burn this. I am Miller Strong, I am going out to change the world one person at a time and I am starting with myself. I am giving myself permission to live again. There is no turning back, I am going for it."

With a smile on my face, I walked out the door, ready for the launch party.

***

The launch party was absolutely incredible. Nearly 500 people came out to the event to support it. We had food, Miller Lite beer in honor of Chad Miller, and his favorite snacks. There was a slideshow honoring Chad's life. Chad had been cremated years before, but I'd never done anything with his ashes. I brought them with me and kept them in the players box we had previously built for the center in his memory years prior. I gave a passionate speech on stage telling Chad's story. I talked about how we owed it to our children and ourselves to honor their legacy and give ourselves permission to live on purpose. That we owed it to our children and ourselves to heal the pains of our past. I told Amber McFarland's story. I shared how it's horrible to lose a child, but it's even worse to have a child disappear and have no closure.

The entire day was a celebration of his life and our bigger mission to help the world with the launch of the Foundation. Everyone there felt something. Tears, laughter, joy, gratitude, resolve, and vision were all shared. It was a smash success. Everyone left as a hero committed to making a difference in the world. I couldn't have been happier. It was an incredible way to re-write the story of my son.

When I left the event that night, I could not have been any happier. My body felt like it was bursting with joy. I was emotionally and physically exhausted from the night, but euphoric.

After the event ended, my boyfriend James and I stayed in Portage at a dear friend of mine's place that was also on my Board of Directors.. It was the first time in years that I went to bed and felt completely in control of my life again. Everything was perfect. The party had been a huge success and I couldn't be happier. I fell asleep smiling.

Yet, I had no idea when I went to sleep that night that I'd wake up to a terrible catastrophe coming right at me.

Chapter 18

I woke up the next morning with that "all is well" glow. It felt like it was going to be an incredible day. I was still on a high from the night before. . We popped open a bottle of champagne and enjoyed the warm water of the hot tub. The sun was lighting her yard perfectly and reflecting of the morning dew in the most peaceful way.

While we were hanging out, enjoying the moment, my friend looked at me and said she needed to talk to me immediately. She'd just received a very disturbing message. Her whole demeanor changed in an instant.

"Erin," she said. Her voice was serious. "You need to go see the psychiatrist at the Portage Clinic right away or the police are coming to pick you up and take you to Eden Mental Health Centre."

"What?!" I asked. My jaw dropped. I was completely confused.

"I don't know, Erin," she said. "They said something about your launch last night being a disaster."

"A disaster? What are you talking about?" I asked. "It was a huge success!"

My mind was racing. My heart started pounding. What the hell was going on? Is someone out to get me? Where is this coming from? This has to be some giant mistake.

"Did you think the launch party was a disaster?" I asked my boyfriend James.

"Of course not! I thought it was fantastic," he replied.

I could sense some conflict in my friend's eyes. She wasn't at the launch, so we were all confused. However, I felt like she'd been privy to information on that phone call that she wasn't telling me.

It was quiet for a few moments. Then she said, "Maybe there are some people you shouldn't trust ."

My eyebrows raised. "What do you mean?" I asked.

"I don't know who you can trust, Erin."

"Look," I said. "I'm not going to the clinic and I'm not going anywhere.. I don't live here. I don't work here. I don't doctor here. I live in Winnipeg. I'm not doing any of those things. It's fucking ridiculous."

"Erin," she said. "They're not giving you a choice."

I didn't know what to do so I called my life coach, Dr. Johnson, who I'd been working with for the past few months. I told her about the party and the insane accusations the psychiatrist was making. She said it sounded like a big misunderstanding. She recommended I go voluntarily and get it sorted out. I agreed, but I asked her to stay right beside her phone so I could get the psychiatrist on the phone, so she could hear, direct from Dr. Johnson, all of the work we had been doing together.

My friend, James, and I hopped in the car and drove to the Portage Clinic together to meet the psychiatrist. We were led into her office. The three of us sat down across from her. It almost felt like I was summoned to the principal's office in middle school. It was absurd.

"Erin, do you have any idea why you're here?" the psychiatrist asked. She sat in a highbacked leather chair, with her legs crossed, her bangs partially in her eyes, with a lined notepad and a pen on her lap.

I looked her dead in the eye. "I have NO idea why I am here."

"You appeared over confident at your launch party last night," she responded.

It literally took my breath away. "Are you fucking serious?" I thought. It had literally taken every ounce of confidence I ever had to get up and deliver that speech about my son last night. And now this psychiatrist was making accusations because I was confident?

"There is also some concern with how much food you had there. There was a random priest giving blessings and I hear you are getting songs produced from Chad's journal." she continued.

"Hold on," I said. "Were you there last night? Because I don't remember seeing you there."

"No," she responded. "I wasn't there, but I've had many people from the community contact me this morning about your behavior at your son's foundation party."

I didn't believe her. I pressed her. "You actually had people call you from the community, all before 10:30am this morning, about my behavior at my son's launch party for Miller Strong?"

"Erin," she tried to play it cool. "I've had a lot of colleagues come to me and talk to me about your behavior."

She started questioning me on everything. She questioned my confidence, she questioned why we had so much food at the party, she actually told me that my "little foundation is a delusion of your imagination. You're having grandiose thinking that you can change the world one person at a time and you're not well."

I wanted to get up and walk out. She was so condescending.

"I can assure you this is not a delusion of anyone's imagination," I sternly replied. "The person that enabled me to start and register the charity with Revenue Canada is your colleague down the hall Dr. Gousseau. Go ask him. Go talk to him."

I continued, "You need to call my counselor Dr. Johnson. Talk to her."

She ignored what I said. Instead, she bombarded me with questions. Every time I would answer, she'd bring up a new one. She asked me what I was doing for self-care. I told her yoga. She then asked me how I could pay for yoga. I told her I sold my house. She then said that I should get a job. I told her my job was the Foundation I just launched and I had been picking up contract work for marketing.

It went on and on. It didn't matter what I had to say, she would just rebuttal and ask a new question. It didn't make any sense.

At one point she asked me to leave the room. She wanted to speak privately with my friend . I thought this was extremely strange. James and I left the room.

While James and I were waiting in the lobby, I saw one of my former colleagues, a man that was supposed to be helping me (a man that had agreed to record the first song from Chad's journal), go into the room along with his wife . My heart sank. I knew this was not good. I had been warned not to be too trusting of anyone except myself.

My boyfriend James turned to me and said, "Erin, look at me. Look at me."

I looked up at him.

"You are getting fucked over, " he said.

"No, it will be alright. I'm not getting fucked over. Things will be okay," I said, just to make myself feel better about the situation. He told me to take off my rose-colored glasses just for a couple minutes.

"Erin, you need to listen to me right now," his voice was absolute. "Your life is getting fucked over right now. You need to get back in there. They are making decisions without you. Go back in there. Answer the questions as simply as you can. One, two, yes, no. Whatever it takes. You need to get back in there and handle this and then we need to get the fuck out of here."

He was right. I realized I was getting fucked over.

I called my mom. I told her that the psychiatrist might call her. I was going to ask the psychiatrist to call my next of Kin - my Mother, Mona. I warned my Mom that the physiatrist may try to convince her that I was crazy . My mom knows I'm not crazy. She helped me plan the whole launch party. Miller Strong was reuniting our family. Giving us all purpose, legacy, family, change, hope and love. I told her not to be worried. That I would be okay.

James and I were called back into the room after their private meeting about me. When we returned, it was just the psychiatrist and the two of us in the room.

"Erin," the psychiatrist began. "I have so much collaborative evidence against you that I'm going to Form 4 you under the Mental Health Act."

"What?" I asked, shocked. "What the hell does that mean?"

"You have two choices, Erin," she responded. "You either have to go back on these prescription medications or I'm bringing the police here to pick you up and take you to Eden Mental Health Centre. If you want the doctors to take you seriously then you need to start listening to my advice."

I didn't know what to say. I was scared, angry, hurt, betrayed, all at the same time. Was she thinking straight? She wanted to detain me for being confident at the launch party of my son's foundation? I could not believe what I was hearing. I knew what she was doing was completely wrong. She had been messing with me for a long time, all the way to my group sessions years before. But I never thought it was this bad.

Of course, I agreed to the prescriptions over having my freedom taken away. I had planned to leave for San Francisco the next day because I had meetings planned to raise awareness for the Foundation. I also had a series of trips planned to New York and to Bali in the weeks following my California trip. The psychiatrist told me all of it was out the window and I was not allowed to go.

I convinced her to allow me to go to San Francisco and meet with her the following Friday as long as I took all the prescriptions. I had to cancel the other trips.

James and I left the office and went straight to my parent's house. I told them what had happened and they couldn't believe it. The entire allegations were ludicrous. I had worked so hard to get off of those prescriptions before. They had made me feel horrible and there was absolutely no way I was getting back on them. I had agreed to the prescriptions just so I could get out of there.

Around this same time, an old friend of mine, Lynn, came back into my life. She and I had a falling out a few months before and never reconciled. My Mom then shared with me what had happened at the launch party the day before. Lynn called my mom directly the afternoon of the launch and asked where she was. My Mom was at the community center setting up for the party. Lynn showed up there a couple minutes later and said, "Mona,   Erin needs an intervention and you need to be the one to do it." My mom told her to get lost. She was grateful to finally have her daughter back. She told Lynn to take a hike.

Lynn then went to my Dad and tried the same thing, but he wouldn't talk to her. Apparently, Lynn was working alongside the psychiatrist. There was some sort of collaboration. I felt betrayed. Even though Lynn and I had a falling out, I never thought she would maliciously go behind my back like this.

I knew I had to draw in my circle of friends and confide in only those people I could trust. I called my friend Lori McFarland who had been spearheading the Miller Strong Foundation with me. She was shocked when I told her what happened. When I told my closest circle of friends and advisors, they all couldn't believe what was happening. They said my speech at the launch party had been incredible. And they were all worried that somehow the psychiatrist would figure out a way to legally lock me up. They could feel the sinister nature of the events that were unfolding. Honestly, I couldn't make this stuff up if I wanted to.

I tried my best to convince everyone that it would all be okay, that the Foundation wouldn't be jeopardized, and that justice would prevail. I didn't know how I had found myself in this situation. I had pulled myself out of the ashes of the death of my son and put myself back together only to be attacked and maligned for doing so.

One week later, I was scheduled to meet with the psychiatrist again at the Portage Clinic. This time I brought my friend Lindsay with me.

As we were walking towards the entrance, I saw the pastor from the local church.

I smiled and waved him down and said, "Let's get a picture with my golden basket in front of the clinic sign."

He agreed and we snapped a quick picture.

After we took the photo, I got this strange feeling like I knew what was going to happen that day. I turned to the pastor after we took the photo and pointed to the clinic and said, "These guys think because I became a Christian and started a Foundation, they think I'm crazy. Watch. I'm going to get detained today."

I walked into the clinic. I had dressed nicely. My hair was on point. People in the community liked me. I had re-kindled my purpose. I knew all of those things bothered the psychiatrist.

In the lobby, there were a lot of people there that were interested in what I was doing. Apparently, I was the talk of the town. People wanted to get pictures with me and my golden basket.

Afterwards, I walked into the psychiatrist office. I took a seat across from her. She sat in her leather chair and I took a seat on the pleather couch with Lindsay on my left. I knew it would be the interview of my life.

"Erin," she started. "I'm assuming you're mad at me that I made you cancel your trips."

"No, I'm not mad at you," I said. "I just want to get my name cleared so I can move on with my life."

She smirked and made a snide comment about my clothes and my basket.

She continued, "I have to agree with what your dad said…that you are currently at your baseline prior to losing Chad."

Baseline means how you are when you start to get help with your trauma.

"Whoa, whoa, whoa," I said firmly. "Why did you call my dad? You are NOT allowed to call him without my permission. That is a breach of confidentiality."

She brushed it aside and continued. "Your dad didn't tell you I called him?"

"No. I've been seeing you for three and a half years and not once has my dad ever been a part of my health initiative at all. You know that losing Chad was equally hard on my Dad and I didn't want him ever knowing just how hard things were for me. You are not allowed to call him and talk to him about those things."

"Erin," she responded. "I called your mom and she wasn't home. So, I talked to your dad."

"Again, you are not allowed to do that," I said, firmly.

"I don't like how you're talking to me, Erin," she forcefully replied.

We sat in silence, staring at each other for a few minutes.

"Erin, I have a lot of evidence that you need urgent psychiatric intervention," she said.

"But you just told me that you agree with what my dad had said and I know he said that I was totally fine. Our foundation has investors, lawyers, accountants, etc.," I replied.

I continued, "Look, this whole thing is a big misunderstanding. Let's just call it what it is – a misunderstanding – and go our separate ways."

"No, you need urgent psychiatric intervention," she glared at me as she said it.

"Actually, I am requesting a second opinion. I am demanding a second opinion right now," I replied firmly.

"Fine, I will send you to a friend of mine within Southern Health-Sante Sud ," she said.

"With all due respect, I am not going to your friend and I am not going to Southern Health because you guys have continued to breach my confidentiality. Last time I was here I saw another doctor go into your office and discuss this with you. Again, breaching my confidentiality agreement. It's unprofessional. What is going on here?" I said.

"I don't like how you're talking to me, Erin."

"Look," I said. "I've been here for 40 minutes and you've yet to ask me a single question about the prescription you tried to put me on. I would think if there really were a valid psychiatric evaluation needed, that would be one of the first things you would ask."

None of this made any sense. I was going to make her prove herself. It felt like a battle of wills.

"Erin, you need an urgent psychiatric intervention. You are no longer allowed to drive. This discussion is over."

By this time, my friend Lindsay was going to leave to get back to work, so I called another friend, Penny, to drive me.

I looked at the physiatrist and said, "This is not right. You know this is not right. I do not need this. I am refusing to go. I am agreeable to getting a second opinion but there is no urgency to this. You just let me go to California.. There is nothing wrong with me, absolutely nothing wrong with me. I've been able to overcome so many challenges that most people can't. You've been working with me for 3 and a half years and seen all of this, and how I've pulled myself out of this situation. In fact, you discharged me out of your care and the only thing that is different now is that I believe in God."

"Erin," her voice was cold and absolute. "You have grandiose thinking. I am going to Form 4 you according to the Mental Health Act."

She wanted to have me detained. This was insane.

"With all due respect, are you sure you want to do that? Because I'm going to tell you right now that this is not going to end well for either one of us. Because if you put me in a situation again where I am locked in a hospital my PTSD is going to come back up again. I have worked so hard to get over this," I said. "Do not do this."

She said nothing.

"This isn't going to end well for you," I continued. "You haven't listened to one word I've been saying to you. You have yet to actually talk to my mother. You're still not listening to me and you're not listening to my family. I don't know if it's Lynn telling you things, or my former colleagues, but you're listening to somebody else, and you need to be listening to us."

With that same coldness she looked right in my eyes and said, "We know what we're talking about, Erin."

There was nothing I could do to change her mind in that moment.

"I'm going to Form 4 you now, Erin," she continued. "I need you to go sit in the lobby and wait there. The RCMP will come to pick you up soon."

I couldn't believe it. "Are you absolutely sure you want me to go sit in the lobby of the clinic and have the police come take me out of this place in public sight of everyone?" I asked, incredulously.

"Yes."

I stood up and walked out of her office.

Chapter 19

I sat in the lobby , in full public view of all of the other patients, as I waited for the police to show up. I knew I was going to get detained, just as I'd said it would before I walked into this ridiculous meeting.

My friend Lindsay was with me and I told her to go find Dr. Ross, because he was one of the few doctors that I trust. But she looked at me and said, "Erin you can leave. Why don't you just get up and walk out?"

I looked at her. "Lindsay, I can't leave. I'm detained. I'm freaking detained under the Mental Health Act. They're not going to let me walk right out of here."

Form 4 is a severe act. It is for people that are in danger to themselves or somebody else. I was disgusted that it had come down to this. I clearly was no danger to anybody, other than the medical establishment wanting to protect its own ass for these bogus claims against me.

There were about 50 people in the lobby area where I was waiting. Almost everyone knew me. People were taking my picture. People were crying when they heard what was happening to me as I sat there waiting for the police to come.

As if all of that wasn't enough, the strangest thing happened. I felt my phone buzzing in my Golden Basket. I pulled it out and it was from my boyfriend James, who lived in New York, calling me. We'd met on Tinder when I was in New York a few months before and had been visiting each other back and forth ever since. He was with me when I'd last met with the psychiatrist, so I knew he was filled in somewhat with what had been going on.

I answered the phone, expecting to hear his voice, when instead it was a woman on the phone.

"I'm going to fucking kill you," I heard a woman say.

"What?" I replied. I had no idea what was going on.

"I'm Darwin's wife," the lady on the phone replied.

"Who is Darwin?" I ask. I'm so confused.

"My husband. The man you've been seeing. Did he tell you his name was James?" The venom in her voice is thick.

Oh my God, I thought. James is not James? And he's married? What the hell is going on?

Right as the shock of this new discovery hit me, I looked up to see the police walking into the medical center to take me away.

I couldn't make this stuff up if I wanted too.

I stammered on the phone as I tried to make sense of all of this while I watched the police walk towards me. "Well, uh, I'm really sorry, but honestly, I'm going to tell you, I'm a really good person. I had no idea that he is married or that his name is Darwin. I would never do that in a million years."

She didn't care. "Did you even know we have kids?" she said with disgust.

Oh fuck. I couldn't believe this. This was too much to take in.

The police were looking for me.

"Look, I can't talk to you right now. I'll talk to you in the next couple of days, but I can't talk right now. I'm really sorry," I said. I hung up the phone.

The police started asking the receptionist for "an Erin Miller" but they don't know to look for me because I wasn't causing a scene. I'm not a crazy person. I was just sitting there in my chair.

One of the receptionists pointed at me. The police walked over.

"Are you Erin Miller?" one of the officer's asked.

"Yes," I looked up at him.

"My name is Chad," the officer stated.

I smile. Of course the officer's name was Chad. I felt a weight lift from me in that moment. I knew that no matter what happened I would be okay. I knew there was some bigger purpose to all of this.

"Is there any chance, Officer, that you can go and talk to Dr. Ross because someone needs to let my family know that I'm okay," I said to Officer Chad.

"Why don't we go talk to him together?" the officer said.

I waited in a small room with the police. Lindsay and Penny were with me too. We were waiting for Dr. Ross & the physiatrist to arrive. By this time the police were feeling a little confused. I'd handed them my business card so they knew who I was and they were pretty puzzled as to why they were there for me in the first place.

The wait seemed to last forever. Strangely enough, when we were all wondering if Dr. Ross and the psychiatrist were going to show up, my dad walked in and said, "My name is George Miller. This is my daughter Erin and you're not going to take her anywhere."

The police looked at him strangely.

"I talked to the psychiatrist on the phone on Sunday," my dad continued. "She called my house at 1:30 in the afternoon. We talked for 43 minutes. She assured me that this was all a misunderstanding and she was going to look after this. I told her that it was absolutely ridiculous the accusations she was making and some sort of scandal that was happening against Erin and that the psychiatrist needed to be the one to fix this. She assured me she would. I don't know what's going on here, but this is not happening."

A few minutes later the psychiatrist walked into the room. My dad got up and walked over to her.

"I'm George Miller, Erin's dad," he said.

The psychiatrist wouldn't look him in the eye. She wouldn't even acknowledge him.

My dad continued asking her questions about the conversation they'd had on the phone over the weekend, over the absurdity of the situation. She just continued to ignore him.

When she finally spoke, it was to one of the questions my Dad had asked, "Where will she be in 24 hours?"

She had no idea.

She continued, "The police have to take her to the Portage Hospital where she will stay in a holding area until we can get her an urgent psychiatric bed."

It was absurd.

My friend Lindsay jumped in. "There's no way you need to take her to the Portage Hospital with two policemen sitting next to her! She is the former Executive Director of the Portage Hospital Foundation. This is not fair. Are you trying to be cruel?"

I turned to everybody in the room including the psychiatrist. "Look, you guys know that my confidentiality has been breached. I do not live in this area. I live in Winnipeg and if this is really happening, then someone needs to send me where I live, not here, it's not right."

The police looked at each other and said, "Alright. You live in Winnipeg. We'll take you there."

"Thank you," I said.

I turned back to the psychiatrist and asked, "What is the reason that I'm being Form 4-ed?"

She stumbled over her words and couldn't give me a real answer. She said that she had no idea where I'd be in 24, 36 or 72 hours. She signed the paper and told the police they could take me away.

I was still in shock as I was escorted out of the room with an officer on each side of me. Dozens of people were looking at me as I walked out of the clinic that I'd raised millions of dollars for. It was humiliating. I took one last look back before I walked out the front doors. I saw the staff of the clinic crying, others were staring in shock, and others taking pictures of the moment. Some people were probably laughing too, I'm sure.

I had to laugh at the absurdity of it all. Years before when I was truly struggling mentally in the aftermath of my son's death, I might have been closer to to needing a psychiatric bed then. But now, with my purpose surer than ever, I was only clear headed. Yet, here I was under detainment.

I was put in the back of the police car, with my Golden Basket sitting next to me. I could hear people pleading with the police through the window of the back seat: "You can't take her away. This is wrong! This has to be a misunderstanding. I don't understand what's wrong!" My mom had arrived by then and was crying and pleading with the police.

But even her pleas wouldn't sway them. They were only following their orders. The officers got in the car and the three of us drove away.

Chapter 20

My parents hopped in their cars and followed the police to where they were taking me. They took me to the Emergency Department at the Health Science Center. Once we arrived, I waited with my family for hours before I was allowed to talk to someone. The longer I sat there, the more I could feel my PTSD being triggered by the tragedy of what was happening around me.

They checked me in and took my normal clothing, my jewelry and all of my belongings and put them away. They gave me a uniform to wear. I sat in the holding area for hours. 4 different people came in to interview me. I answered all of their questions. I told the same story to them over and over again. After hours and hours of being there, I asked point blank, "Can I leave now?"

"No," the interviewer said. "Form 4 means we have to hold you against your will for 72 hours."

"What?" I said. "Can't I just talk to someone? This is really ridiculous."

I felt like all of my rights as a human had been violated. It was humiliating. I had been forced here against my will and under false pretenses. I wasn't allowed to go outside (which had been a major part of my healing process).

At some point I realized I really had to watch what I was saying, because they would use anything against me. So, I sat in my holding area praying and meditating, doing my best to keep calm. I had no idea what they were recording or planning to use against me. I had to watch what I said or did.

They put me in a lock down unit. The room was #17 - yet another sign I was going to be okay. There were a couple of patient rooms, some interview rooms, and a room to have a shower. The interviews seemed to be non-stop rotating from one staff member to the next as they questioned me. They made me relive the experience of losing Chad over and over and over again. It was horrible.

There was a little lounge area across from the nursing station where I would sit and eat my meals. I would look out the big windows hoping that I would be released soon so I could leave these terrible people behind and go to Indonesia. Spending time outside had been a critical part of my healing. When I asked to go outside they denied me and said I could look out the window. When I asked if I could attend the church service, they denied me. I could feel the old fears slowly creeping back into my heart.

After being there for close to 72 hours, I finally got to talk to a psychiatrist. Up to that point, I'd only been interviewed by the physician assistants, nurses, students, and nursing staff. I felt like it was the interview of my life. Keep in mind, after 72 hours in holding, I *still* had not been told why I am there.

I asked the physiatrist, "I'd like to know what they're saying about my situation. Nobody has told me why I'm being held here under Form 4. All I know is that I've been told I have 'grandiose thinking,' I'm overconfident and I spent too much money on my son's foundation party.'"

He said, "I'm here to figure out what's going on."

He spent the next hour asking me questions about the Miller Strong Foundation, about my son Chad, about my recovery from his passing, about the therapists I'd worked with and a bunch of other things.

He took notes the whole time and eventually said, "Okay, well, I'm going to discharge you with no follow up, unless of course you ever feel like you need some sort of help. Here's the number to call in Winnipeg and make sure you have a family doctor registered."

I couldn't believe it.

"So, I can go?" I asked.

"Yes," he replied. "Go live whatever kind of life you like, because you deserve it."

And just like that I was a free woman again.

Chapter 21

My mom was there to pick me up when I was released. I will never forget walking through those doors and breathing a sigh of relief as I walked out. The sunshine hit my face and I breathed fresh Manitoba air. I said a prayer of relief and gratitude, "Thank you God for getting me out of there."

As soon as I got out, I called my lawyer and told him what had happened. He advised me that I would have a very difficult time winning a direct case, and it would cost me a fortune. Instead, he advised me to put in a complaint to the Manitoba College of Physicians and Surgeons to begin an internal investigation. I explained to him that in my mind I had already won. I had been released. I still had no idea why I had been Form 4-ed or what they'd put on my chart. I just knew the whole thing was morally wrong and probably criminal.

After I submitted a formal complaint, I felt like I needed to continue moving forward with my life. I had made a promise to myself to honor Michelle's memory by scuba diving in Bali and Indonesia. I still intended to go, so I quickly re-organized my plans so that I could travel. Two days later I was on a plane.

My first destination was a tiny little island off the coast of Indonesia called Gili Trawangan. It was the exact opposite of my life back home in Manitoba. It was warm, tropical, and lush. There was fresh fruit everywhere, perfect sand beaches, and crashing waves.

As I explored the small island that first day, somehow, I found myself on a beach called "God's Beach." It also ended up being Michelle's birthday. As I sat on the sand with her scuba diving gear next to me, I was overwhelmed with gratitude and the serendipity of it all. 96 hours before, I had been in a mental institution in Manitoba, falsely detained. And now here I was, on "God's Beach" in Indonesia, on Michelle's birthday, about to scuba dive in her memory. I felt this overwhelming sense of gratitude to God for this moment and all that I'd been able to overcome. I put on my gear and submerged myself in the water. It was one of the most beautiful dives of my entire life.

***

Spending time in Indonesia gave me time to really reflect and slow down. I knew this was the time that God had given to me to really get to know myself and reflect on who I am, where I'm going, and how I want to show up in the world going forward.

From the moment my foot hit the sand on those beaches I felt instantly at peace. I fell in love with the place. It was absolute paradise. There were no cars. You could only walk or ride a bike. The locals were incredibly friendly and generous. It really gave me the space to slow down and heal.

One morning, I woke up early to catch the sunrise over the island mountains. The sun broke over the mountain skyline, lighting up the sky in brilliant orange and pink. It was the most beautiful sunrise I'd ever seen. A few minutes later, a short, smiling local comes walking down the beach.

"It's magnificent," he said, looking at the sunrise and then smiling at me.

"Absolutely," I nodded and smiled.

We got to chatting and he introduced himself as Ricky. We ended up going to grab breakfast afterwards. He told me he worked as a beach boy at a local bar. A few months earlier, there had been a massive earthquake that had caused damage to a lot of the local structures. They were re-building the local bar and cleaning up the beach. I asked him to take me to see the bar.

I ended up meeting the owner of the bar and chatting with him for hours. They were having a lot of problems with rebuilding after the earthquake and I told him that I could help him bring the bar back to life and make it buzz again. The bar didn't have a name, so we ended up calling it the Miller Strong 17 Bar.

We painted the sign, cleaned the beach up, and made it an incredible place to hang out. People started to flock to the bar. Business was so good that we needed people to start working there, so it was providing locals jobs as well. The location was incredible. You could go snorkeling right out front of it, or grab a paddleboard, and even swim with the local sea turtles.

I felt like Ricky was Chad re-incarnated in a way. We had this near-instant connection. He would even say things that Chad and I would say to each other like, "I love you long time." The first time he said it, I started crying. Chad and I always said that to each other. It was yet another example of God's provision and care for me. I knew I was on my right path.

***

When Michelle and I had originally planned our travels here, we had talked about investing in the area for retirement. I had a contact for a man named Danny, who could help me with that. The only problem was I had no idea where to find him. While I was walking around town one day, I passed a place called "The Jungle." It was a little bar. I saw a man standing on the platform having a great time dancing in there. I got this strange hunch that this was exactly who I was looking for. I walked right up to him and introduced myself. He said his name was Danny and that he was the person I'd wanted to talk too.

We chatted about what would need to happen to invest in the area. There was something about him that drew me to him, and I could tell the same was happening for him. After we discussed a bit of business, Danny invited me to hang out with him on the beach. We ended up going to a party later that night, and then we started dating.

If you would have asked me a week before if that was the situation I'd have found myself in, I'd have said, "No way in hell!" But then again, I didn't think that my now lying ex-boyfriend "James" was married with children either, so I was free to do what I wanted.

Danny was worth it though. He was so sweet and kind to me. After all of the heartbreak I'd been through with Chad, with pulling myself out of the ashes, with being detained and finding out the truth about "James," my heart had been shattered so many times. Danny was a special man to make my heart open up so quickly.

I remember Danny saying to me one day after we'd been hanging out for weeks, "Erin, you are the most beautiful woman I have ever met."

I laughed it off. He couldn't possibly be serious.

He could see that I didn't believe him. He persisted, "Erin, I'm serious. Look in the mirror."

"No, Danny," I nervously laughed. "I don't look in the mirror."

"You don't look in the mirror?" he asked, confused.

"No, I don't look in the mirror," I replied.

Danny stood there and calmly said, "Erin, look at yourself. Look how beautiful you are. You're like a shining light everywhere you go."

From then on, everywhere we'd go, he'd show me that I was treating people differently than everyone else. He showed me that people were attracted to me, and that they would naturally respond to me and smile.

I don't think I'd ever noticed this about myself before, but it felt really good to have someone else see that in me. I felt like I was seeing myself again and loving myself for who I am and what I bring to the world. Danny helped me see the natural light inside of me and I started to fall deeply for him.

***

With each passing day on the Island, I felt my mind growing calmer and calmer and my intuition getting stronger. I began to feel in sync with the natural rhythm of life for the first time in forever. I was diving regularly and enjoying growing the community with the Miller Strong 17 Bar.

One day I headed out to go diving. On my way there, my gut told me not to go. It told me to go sit down on a particular spot on the beach near a palm tree. As I sat under the tree, I looked over at this girl sitting nearby. She had blonde hair, sun kissed skin, a slight, beautiful completion, and a gorgeous smile. Her name was Lucy. We started chatting. She told me her name was Lucy and she's from Europe. She was in a horrific car accident and was on life support for months. The doctors told her mom that she wasn't going to live, yet here she was strong, and recovered and learning to be a certified yoga instructor.

I shared with her a bit about my own journey and what we created with the Miller Strong Foundation. She immediately told me she wanted to help however she can.

She had a book sitting by her side with a train ticket sticking out of it that she was using as her bookmark. On the corner of the train ticket I saw the date of August 20th on it – Chad's birthday. It was all too serendipitous. I couldn't believe it. It was yet another sign.

I looked at the girl again and noticed something that I hadn't caught at first. There was a glow about her, like she was radiating this subtle, yet powerful beauty. I told her that and she said, "Haha, that's because I'm blessed!"

I laughed.

Lucy and I ended up grabbing lunch together. While we were chatting and having a few cocktails and food on the beach, a striking woman approached and said to us, "I am a mermaid." She looked like a mermaid. She was incredibly beautiful. She looked like she was a model.

We got talking about what we were all doing on this island, and eventually she said, "Actually, I was just visiting with my spiritual healer. It changed my life."

"Really?" I asked. "I've been wanting to go to a spiritual healer. I just don't know which one to go to or who to trust. There are thousands of them."

She looked right into my eyes and said, "You need to connect with my spiritual healer."

All of it was too perfect for me not to trust her. My intuition telling me to sit next to this tree, meeting this beautiful lady, Chad's birthday on the bookmark, and now a recommendation for a spiritual healer to help me on my journey.

Within an hour I had made all of the arrangements for a visit to the spiritual healer. Little did I know how that this man would completely alter and save my life.

Chapter 22

After a massive goodbye party from my new friends on Gilli T Island, I hopped on a boat a few days later to meet my new spiritual healer/ teacher on the mainland. His name was Vas Golden, the man who would completely change my life. I had no idea what to expect when I got on that boat. All I knew was that I was following my instincts and that I was being led to this man for a reason.

On my way there, my faith was tested. For reasons unknown to me, my bank card stopped working a day or so before I left to meet Vas. I essentially had no access to money and still needed to make my way back to Canada after the meeting with him. Even though my mind was freaking out about how I was going to survive, my soul kept trusting that everything would work out and God would provide me with exactly what I needed along the way.

And that's exactly what happened. Every step of the way, the right person would come along and help me to get exactly where I needed to go. Even my driver that Danny had arranged for me had a Canada Flag on the rearview mirror of his car when he picked me up. Each step of the way, I was given little nudges that I was going in the right direction.

When I finally made it to Vas Golden's place, I felt exhausted, yet excited. The weight of everything that I had been through over the years, from Chad's death, to my emotional pain, to being detained, to the death of my friend, all seemed to roar to life inside of me when I arrived. In retrospect, I think it was all coming to the forefront of my awareness so it could finally be healed with the help of this man.

Vas Golden had an incredible aura about him. He was kind and loving, yet reverent and grounded at the same time. I could tell immediately that there was something powerful and special about him. He had long, shoulder length blackish brown hair that was starting to get gray in places and eyes that could see right into your soul. His hair was cut in a mullet like fashion. He wore a necklace with a stone and a gold ring with a ruby in it. He had a heart of gold and I knew my time with him would be sacred. And so our work began. I spent seven days with him. It was hell and heaven all at the same time.

The day of our work began with an early morning. After breakfast, we sat outside and talked almost the entire day. I told him about the trauma I had had my entire life. Between Vas and his lovely wife, they explained everything in detail in terms of what they could provide healing for me at Randim Bali, the name of their home/sanctuary.

The next day Vas ordered flowers and coconut to be delivered. I was to have 3 separate healings, a protection ceremony and then we were going to call Chad. If it sounds strange to you, it was to me as well, but

I knew that God had guided me to this man and I was completely surrendered to whatever I was meant to learn, heal, or experience.

Vas wrote my name on a piece of paper and smudged it with special oil. A large stick of incense sat burning in front of him, with soft wafts of the incense smoke passing over him. Once the incense was completely burned out, I lay on the bed completely open to taking all my pain and suffering away.

As the work began, I felt so much pain being pulled out of my body. I was shaking profusely and could see Vas sweating. I kept my eyes closed and let the process happen. It took hours, but once he was done, he laid down adjacent to me. He was soaking wet from sweating so much and he looked at me and told me I was a sick girl. I said, "I told you so."

After laying there for a while, I opened my eyes and I felt like I could literally see again. I had no idea I couldn't see before, but everything in my world seemed brighter, like the colors were turned up. Everything looked amplified, like going from a black and white TV to all of the sudden seeing in high definition 4K on the latest TV technology available.

Vas asked me to drink the coconut water from the blessed coconut that was delivered to us earlier in the day. I then poured the flowers that he had blessed over the crown of my head then worked my way down my entire body. We were both exhausted and I went to bed.

In the morning, I woke up and enjoyed Bajawa coffee (a special native coffee) and was feeling like I could breathe again. Vas decided to do the next two healings over the next two days. After each one you could see the physical transformation in my body. My skin seemed more vibrant. My eyes came back to life. I felt lighter each day. Every healing seemed easier as he was helping me release so much pain and suffering out of my broken body.

On the fifth day I received a protection ceremony. He went through my whole life with me as I lay there and asked me to think about every rotten thing that had happened to me. He did it in stages of my life. The only way I can describe this it was like a black and white TV that is fuzzy with static, trying to capture the picture signal, and as I let go of more things it became clearer and clearer. I could literally feel all the traumatizing memories leaving my body.

This surprised me, but the hardest thing to let go of was that I had an abortion when I was 17, the year after I gave birth to Chad. In the whole story of my life, that was the toughest thing to forgive myself for because it was the hardest decision I had ever made in my life. When I had to have the abortion I said to my best friend Lindsay, "There won't be anything harder than this in my life." I guess I was partially right.

After that ceremony, the old Erin Miller died, and the new Erin Miller was born.

On the 6th day we called Chad. Vas explained to me what was going to happen. He explained that he would be using his knowledge to call Chad to me. I explained that I was scared because the last time I said goodbye to Chad was when I took him off life support and watched him die in my arms. I regretted every second of that decision.

Vas said, "Well, yes Erin, you said goodbye to his physical body. Now it's time to say goodbye to his soul. He is waiting for you."

I sat on the bed holding hands with Vas as I heard him talking to Chad.

He said, "Chad you have to trust my knowledge and come. I have your Mom here and she really wants to talk to you."

Next thing I knew I could feel Chad in the room. Vas turned me towards where I felt him and I started crying. I couldn't see Chad, but I felt his presence incredibly strong.

Vas told him he doesn't live in the human world anymore. Chad was hungry, tired and cold. He had no idea what had happened to him. He asked me, "Mom, what did I do wrong?"

I said, "Nothing. You did nothing wrong, my sweet boy."

"Why are you crying?" he asked me.

"Because I'm so happy, Chad," I replied, tears dripping down my eyes.

He asked me where Kaeley was. I said she was at school. Then Vas told me I have to let him go.

So I started to explain to him that I need him to go. There were a lot of people waiting for him. It was time for him to go on.

So I started saying goodbye for the last time. Vas kept saying to me you have to say it with your whole heart, because Chad will not leave until he believes you are ready.

"Chad, it's time for you to go. Fly like an Eagle," I said. He was an Eagle. That was his hockey team, the Robert Morris Eagles. "Fly as high as you can and I will look after everything here until I get to heaven to meet you. You are going to a glorious place. God is waiting for you. You won't be hungry, cold or tired ever again. You can visit me in my dreams every night and you can make sure I am going to be okay , you can be your Mom's guardian Angel now, okay Clun?" (that was my nickname for him).

He said, "Okay, Mom. Love you long time." We always said that to each other.

And then that was it. He was gone. I felt his spirit leave. It was over and he was free. The peace and comfort that ran through my veins was instant. I looked at Vas with a sense of overwhelming peace and joy and smiled, "This could be a movie..."

He laughed.

***

On the 7th day, Vas removed the lumps that were on my breasts. I had suspected I had breast cancer from all the prescription medication that I had been on over the years, yet never confirmed it. It had been affecting my organs to the point of my body shutting down almost completely. However, I did not tell Vas anything about this. He simply knew. They brought in a woman later that day that gave me a special massage and she assured me that my breasts were healed.

The next day I packed up all my stuff, went and met Vas one last time. I was given blessings by his family. He sent a blessed rose with me to sanctify some items in Canada that are special to me. It was an offering, a rare flower found on the mountain top under a full moon. It was a fitting gift to receive as I finished my work with him. I gave him a hug, thanked him for everything he'd done, and left for the airport.

When I got to the airport hotel, I met two women, Eva & Caro. I wasn't supposed to leave until the next day, so we spent a magical day together at the hotel pool. I had never seen true love like these two women had for each other. We instantly bonded and shared our stories. After hearing about Chad, they told me they were going to get matching Miller Strong 17 tattoos.

While sitting poolside, I watched them do a photo shoot at the ocean with my Golden basket. My heart was bursting with joy. As I watched them take photos, I talked to my boyfriend Danny from Gilli T island on the phone. Our love was such an unexpected and unusual one that it confirmed to me that you can fall in love with anyone, even a man from Indonesia that comes from a poor village. The relationship healed my broken heart and allowed me to see that I am good enough, I am special and I am worthy of being and feeling Loved. I love that he calls me his "Darling." That day on the phone, I told him "I love you" for the first time. I felt like my life was complete. I had everything I needed and more.

That last night in Indonesia was magical. I remember walking down to the beach and sitting on the sand, watch the waves crash. My eye was drawn up to the sky. The stars were brilliant that night.

As I gazed at the stars, I remembered that, years before after Chad passed, my best friend Darlene named a star in the sky for Chad. My nickname for Chad was "Clun." She named the star Klun, with a K. I was mad that she spelled his name wrong in the official star registry. Yet, that last night in Indonesia, I found the star in the sky and thought "Klun" was the perfect spelling for his star. It was a combination of Erin & Darlene's love for Chad. I smiled. My heart was so full of gratitude. I knew I could look up at the sky anytime I wanted now and connect with my boy.

[If you ever want to find Chad's star for yourself, here are the details:

Registered Star Klun 108732-6591-3804444 the star with the coordinates

RA: 9h8m52.3s DEC: + 51° 36m17.0s]

I stayed up all night until Chad's star turned in to sunrise and I couldn't see it any longer. Sitting on the beach of the Indian Ocean I watched the sun rise above the mountains. I felt complete gratitude, inner peace, joy and happiness, as the gentle ocean breeze kissed my face and my toes curled into the sand.

It was a fitting way to end my sacred trip to Indonesia. The new Erin Miller was excited, healed, protected, loved, felt inner joy, had wisdom, knowledge and vision and believed wholeheartedly in the power of God. I was exactly where I needed to be and that I am forever grateful for.

Later that day I got on a plane and made the long journey back to Canada where I was looking forward to the adventures of my new life.

Chapter 23

Spending all of this time with Vas Golden and on the islands made me aware of one essential part of my healing journey.

Nature.

In our modern societies it's so easy to disconnect from nature. Yet, nature holds tremendous wisdom. The more in tune with it we are, the more in tune we get with our intuition.

I realized that I'd been led to all of these different wonderful experiences because I was in tune with my intuition and acted on what it was telling me. But I'm certainly not unique in this ability. We all have the ability to tune in to ourselves. That's really what the word "intuition" means. Inner tuning with oneself.

Yet, in our modern world, it's easy to get out of tune and only pay attention to what's going on externally. The problem with that is that it makes us miss tremendous opportunities that are right in front of us.

Nature forces you to quiet down and begin to hear again. It's really hard to do that when you're plugged in to your phone all the time, running around, stressed out, and basically making yourself crazy with all you have to do. That was how I was living my life for years, just trying to survive and rushing from one thing to the next. It was my way of dampening the pain that I was feeling inside.

When I found God, I realized that the more I went inward, listened and prayed, read scripture, the more I was able to see, hear and attract the right opportunities. In the Bible, person after person hears God most clearly when they're in nature. Whether that's the still small voice after the earthquake, or the burning bush in the wilderness, or Jesus going up in to a mountain by himself, nature is a pathway for us to connect with the divine and open our intuition.

If you're struggling to hear yourself, start there. Go for a walk in the woods, get in a paddle boat and sit on the lake, lay in the grass on a hillside. Find simple moments to connect with nature. Get up early and watch the sunrise or watch the sunset.

You deserve it.

Chapter 24

When I returned to Canada, I came back as a different person. Or maybe just a person that I had forgotten about. I came back with a lightness about me that was palpable. The beautiful people I met, the experiences I had, and the deep healing work with Vas Golden all revealed in me something that I'd forgotten about: that bright, shining light inside of me. For the first time in forever, I felt like myself again.

As I was flying back home, I realized I'd found myself again. I found that I was a happy person. I remembered that I was a woman full of love to give the world. I saw that I was a leader who could make big or small change wherever I went. I realized I had found my superpower.

And do you know what my superpower is?

Being me.

And I'd argue that your superpower is being YOU. Not the scared, small, timid you. The happy, loving, fierce, unfearful you. When you remember who you are and live that way, you are UNSTOPPABLE. When you do this, there is no kryptonite that can take you down. You radiate your natural aura of awesomeness.

After I became aware of my own superpower, I had another "aha moment." I'd re-written my story and Chad's, just as I had promised to do all those years before. I'd taken a stand for myself and something greater than me. I'd turned our story into something that made me anew and birthed an idea and organization that would impact people for good.

I believe you can do the same. You don't have to let your past define you. It is our stories about the events that happened – more than the event itself – that defines who we are and what we become. If I had stayed a victim over the loss of my son, instead of using his death as a voice for change in this world, then I would have had nothing to live for. Re-writing the story not only saved me, but it allowed me to help others.

Your deepest pain and darkest moments are stories that are waiting for you to re-write. They have gifts in them, as hard as that may be to see, that will come to life if you allow them. But it all starts in how you choose to look at your past.

What will you stand for? What lesson will you learn from the most difficult moments of your life? And most importantly, how can you turn it into something that helps others? The answers to these questions are all a matter of CHOICE. Each day you are given the gift of Choice by our Creator. You choose how you will respond. You choose how you will show up. You choose how long you will stay knocked down for. You also choose when you will no longer accept being a victim and claim your right to victory.

This starts with loving yourself first. I mean, really loving yourself. I know that can be hard to do, especially when you have crippling grief. I lived in that space for years, beating myself up for not saving Chad, for how I raised him, for believing his choices were my fault. All it did was put me in a cycle of self-hatred for years.

Yet, loving yourself doesn't have to be so complicated or hard. It starts with saying, "I love myself enough to give myself a few minutes a day or an hour a week just for myself." It starts with prioritizing the reality that you matter – because you do! And if no one else tells you that, then let me be the one to tell you that you absolutely do matter.

Take the time for yourself. Go on a walk alone. Spend time in nature. Treat yourself to a bath. Do the hobby that makes you happy. Loving yourself starts with giving yourself space to do the things you love to do.

Do Your Best With What You've Been Given

I believe we are all trying our best most of the time. We all want to do well in life and be kind to other people. We all want to look back on our lives and be proud of who we are. It's just that often times we're so invested in our own stories that our "best" today doesn't mean that is our "best" in 6 months, a year, or two years. But you've got to do your best today in order to get to those future moments.

Right after Chad died, it was all I could do to drag myself out of bed somedays. That was my best at the time. Maybe you're in a similar place. Just strive to be a little bit better and happier than you were yesterday.

I remember asking myself, "Erin, do you think that you did the best you could with what you've been given in this situation?" I knew in my heart the answer was "Yes." If the answer is not yes for you then figure out how to make it a yes. Accept that you have had moments where you are doing your best and resolve to make more of them.

And if you don't feel you can do your best by yourself, then please get help. Don't try and do it alone. We all go through horrible, difficult times. Reach out and find someone to help you through it.

Gratitude

One of the most powerful ways that I've found to put my dark moments in perspective is gratitude. I know gratitude is such a trite and overused concept these days, but it's absolutely worth mentioning here because we are in a gratitude crisis today. With social media constantly making us compare our lives to other people, there has never been more need for moments of sincere appreciation and gratitude for the reality that we are still here. The fact that you are reading this book right now means that you are one of the lucky ones! 150,000 people died on the planet TODAY and you were NOT one of them. You've still got life in you. You've still got more to give. That is worth being grateful for.

And if you're in a dark place, where you're contemplating suicide, first off, please, please, please reach out to someone. Reach out to a Suicide Prevention hotline and just talk to someone. Even though you may not think it, the loss of your life will be devastating. I promise. I would do anything to get my son back. Don't put your family, friends, or coworkers through that. You do matter and I personally want you to live! I know you have gifts to share with the world and I am grateful for you to be here sharing this journey with me.

Purpose & Mastery

My biggest challenge in the aftermath of Chad's death was that I was absorbed with the loss of him. I didn't know how I would go on living and I blamed myself for not doing enough to protect him. It was only when I began to re-write his story and find purpose in my loss that my life began to turn around.

The same is true for you. Life will punch you and knock you down. There's no way around it that I know of. But your strength and your resolve to get through it comes when you find meaning in your suffering. It draws you to life when you turn it into something that helps other people.

Figure out what you are good at then figure out how you're going to do it. That is when you're going to show up the best in this world for yourself and for others. Do what you're really good at. Journaling is a perfect way to start writing down your thoughts and get things put into action.

For example, I'm terrible at drawing. That's not my calling. I am, however, really good at creating experiences for people. That's what I decided to do over and over again through my life. That's why I started the Miller Strong #17 Foundation. That's why I wrote this book. I love creating meaningful experiences for people.

And if you're not yet sure what you're good at, ask your friends, ask yourself, and, most importantly, ask God. He's the Creator after all and gave you your unique gifts. It may not be easy to find out at first, but I promise you it's worth it.

Re-Write Your Story

Shortly after returning to Canada, I was given Chad's spirit name at a traditional First Nations ceremony. The ceremony was led by a man named Kevin from the Aurora Recovery Center – the addiction recovery center I had sent Jason, Chad's biological father, to. Kevin was instrumental in helping Jason begin the process of showing up better for himself and Chad's half-siblings.

During the ceremony Kevin gave Chad the spirit name of Swirling Thunderbird Man from the Buffalo Clan. He told me that Chad was a person who gave himself for others. That he was a man who went down the path less traveled and made sure that people didn't get left behind. His spirit name represents protection and strength.

It was a special moment for me to receive this spirit name for my son. It made me realize that no matter what you go through in life, your name can always be given anew. Your life can be given a new meaning.

That's what this ceremony represented to me and I share it, because, you too, can re-write your story. You can give your life a re-birth, no matter what you've been through or what you're going through.

So, how do you do that? Well, there is a process that's helped me along the way.

1. Accept the Old Story:
Most of us live in a world of denial, doubt, anger or destruction for what's happened to us in the past. Maybe it was our own fault, maybe it wasn't. It doesn't really matter. Our minds live in the past, repeating the

events over and over again. We become slaves to our stories and constantly ask ourselves things like, "Why did this happen?" "If I had only done this or that!"

But those things never change it. The first taste of freedom comes when you fully accept what happened. This is not easy to do, you will not like it, but it is necessary. When I accepted that Chad was dead and that I could do nothing to bring him back, it then gave me the freedom to be able to move forward. Accept what is, no matter how painful. You cannot change it.

2. Learn From the Old Story:

The trauma's and heartaches of our past are painful. I won't sugarcoat that. But hidden inside of tragedy is the seed of something that can benefit the world. Jesus died on the cross. But his sacrifice made way for billions of people to learn from him and come closer to God. That never would have happened without the pain.

When Chad died, I had a choice. Accept it and be bitter and broken forever or learn from it. It took me many years, but eventually I chose to learn from it. I saw that what had happened to him was tragic. I saw my own shortcomings, learned from them, and forgave myself. I forgave Chad. I saw the horrors of the pharmaceutical institutions and the problems they create. All of these taught me something. I could see something that I never would have seen before. I could see real problems that others were facing that I never would have known had this not happened.

3. Write The New Story:

I promised that I would re-write Chad's story – that I would use it for good. I chose to start a foundation, to write this book, to share this message and turn it into something that moved other people. Chad could have been one of millions of kids that overdose on drugs and I could have been another heartbroken parent left to pick up the pieces in the aftermath.

But my son is a great man. I chose to use his life and my life for the benefit of others. This is the true power – the real SECRET – of re-writing your story. When you take the shit in your life and you consciously allow God to use it for something that heals and blesses other people. When you allow this, you transmute garbage into a priceless gift.

If you don't know how to do this with your life experience, that is okay. You don't have to know today. Just accept what is, find the lessons in the past, and humbly ask God, "Show me how I can be a blessing to others. Use my life for good."

That humble prayer, if asked honestly, will always be given an answer.

Your Journey

It's been an honor to share the story of my son Chad. It's been an honor to share my own journey with you. And now it's time for you to embark on your own journey. It's time for you to take a stand for your life. It's time to re-write your story. It's time to find your superpower hidden in the middle of all of the crap that you've been through.

It's hidden in there, believe me. If someone like me can find it, I know you can. And if you're someone who wants extra support along the way, I strongly encourage you to reach out. Send me a direct message on Instagram and ask about one of my mentorship programs to help you move through your own tragedy and find your own superpower. Send me a message and connect with me on Instagram at @erinmariemiller17

I also encourage you to join my free Facebook group and join a community of other likeminded individuals going on their own journey of healing and transformation. Click here to join.

And remember, you do matter. Your life has meaning. Your past does not have to define you. You are worthy of love and you have massive gifts to share with the world. I believe in you.

In finishing, I'd like to leave you with a beautiful song from my friend Lynda-Dobbin Turner called Strong. It was written in honor of Chad Miller. Listen here: https://store.cdbaby.com/cd/lyndadobbinturner4

With love,
Erin Miller
#millerstrong17

About The Author

Erin Miller is the former Executive Director of the Portage District General Hospital Foundation and the founder of Miller Strong #17 Foundation, a non-profit organization committed to making the world better, one person at a time. After the tragic loss of her son, Chad, to a drug overdose, she has been an outspoken advocate for those who have experienced loss, trauma, and tragedy. She has been featured in Global News Canada and the Winnipeg Free Press. An avid scuba diver, when she's not traveling she resides in Manitoba, Canada.

Made in the USA
Middletown, DE
06 March 2020